GAME OF MY LIFE

FLORIDA

GATORS

GAME OF MY LIFE

FLORIDA

GATORS

MEMORABLE STORIES OF GATORS FOOTBALL

PAT DOOLEY

FOREWORD BY URBAN MEYER

SPORTS
PUBLISHING

Library of Congress Cataloging-in-Publication Data is available on file.

ISBN: 978-1-61321-009-3

FOR MY PARENTS, WHO IMMERSED ME IN GATOR
FOOTBALL AT AN EARLY AGE, FOR MY WIFE, WHO
MAKES EVERY DAY SPECIAL, AND FOR MY DAUGHTERS,
WHO MAKE ME WHOLE.

CONTENTS

FOREWORD

When I became the head football coach at the University of Florida, I was well aware of the history of Gator football as it pertained to the incredible run during the 1990s. I watched Steve Spurrier's teams play and admired their abilities to compete and win games.

Once I arrived in Gainesville, it became clear that there was a deeper history to the school's football program. I am a big believer in celebrating the past and embracing the traditions and heroes of previous seasons.

Bringing those players back to speak to our team—Jack Youngblood, Carlos Alvarez, Emmitt Smith, Brad Culpepper, to name a few—helped our team win the 2006 national championship.

During my time at UF, it also has become obvious to me that *Gainesville Sun* sports columnist Pat Dooley has a grip on that history. Pat lived through much of it and has covered so many of the players who have made Florida football special.

In his book *Game of My Life Florida*, Pat takes Gator fans back into time and relives some of the special games in Florida football history, including a very special night for me and my family in Glendale, Arizona, with his chapter on Chris Leak.

The Gator Nation will enjoy looking back on these amazing accomplishments by so many of the people who helped make Florida the place to be in college football.

This book brings to life those games and those players who helped pave the way to many championships and happy times for the Gators.

Enjoy it with me and Go Gators!

There is also a chapter in *Game of My Life* about one of my favorite players— Ahmad Black. Ahmad made a huge play to help us win a second national title in 2008 and made the biggest play of my final game as Florida's coach in the Outback Bowl.

—Urban Meyer
Former Head Football Coach
Florida Gators Football

INTRODUCTION

When I was approached about writing a book detailing the "Game of My Life" for more than two dozen former Gator football players, I was giddy. Heck, I had seen almost all of the great performances in Florida history and knew many of the players involved.

And for a guy who considers deadline writing my best trait, having a year to write it made it seem like a snap.

But a few things happened along the way. In my job as columnist for *The Gainesville Sun*, I couldn't have foreseen the magical runs by the football and basketball teams. Covering the three-peat made my time more difficult to manage.

But with a lot of help, I got it done.

Since I had personal relationships with many of the players I wanted to interview, getting them to sit down for interviews wasn't difficult when I could find the time. Norm Carlson and Steve McClain with Florida's sports information department filled in details and phone numbers.

Jim Trebilcock and Brian Kratzer at *The Sun* helped with the technological aspects of the book.

And my wife, Karen, was incredibly understanding when I told her I was locking myself in the office to write.

Putting this book together was an educational experience. One thing I discovered in talking to this Who's Who of Gator players was how many of them made it to where they are because of two things:

1. Somewhere in their lives there was a mentor, whether it was a coach or a friend or a parent or even a peer group, who helped them with the foundation that allowed them to succeed.

2. They all had a tremendous inner fire that pushed them to be the best. One of my favorite stories involved Neal Anderson, who told his coaches at Florida that he was good enough to start and he'd better start or he was going home. He started against Kentucky and came up with "The Game of His Life."

Memories are certainly faded and I had to provide some prodding with older players. Lindy Infante was the smart one, getting Carlson to send him the play-by-play of the 1960 Georgia Tech game to his Crescent Beach home so his memory would be refreshed when we sat down.

There were a couple of players I called who could not remember any game that stood out. They are not included in this book, but it doesn't mean they weren't great players.

One player whose memory was certainly fresh was Chris Leak. I saw Chris at a function before the 2006 season and told him I'd like to include him in the book after the season was over and his eligibility was up.

As I walked away from Chris, I wondered if there would be a compelling game that would interest the readers. If Florida went 8-4, what would that game be? At LSU in 2003? His first start? One of the Georgia games?

Little did I know that he would have one of the most memorable games of all as MVP of the BCS National Championship Game in Glendale, Arizona.

When I approached Florida coach Urban Meyer about writing the foreword for this book, he asked me if I had any of his players in it.

"Chris Leak," I said.

"What was his game?" Meyer asked.

"What do you think?" I said.

Meyer then asked me if it was Leak's best game. I told him that he had better games statistically, but never a better game.

Some of the choices by the players may surprise you. Shane Matthews, who quarterbacked Florida to its first SEC title, chose his first game as a starter. So did Wayne Peace. James Bates chose his senior season return to Knoxville. Carlos Alvarez chose his return home to Miami as a sophomore.

Others were more obvious—Kerwin Bell's miracle against Auburn, Chris Doering's catch at Kentucky, Danny Wuerffel's national title win in New Orleans, Wilber Marshall's harrassment of USC's backfield.

The thing that I took away from this book more than anything was that I thought I knew just about everything there was to know about Florida football. It turns out I only knew the stuff on the surface.

These pages should give you insight that will surprise you and delight you. I hope so, because as someone who has been going to Gator games since 1962, this was truly a labor of love.

More than anything, I want to thank the players who gave me their time. With every one of them, I told them it would take 20 minutes or so and we always ended up talking for at least an hour.

One funny story before I turn you over to *Game of My Life*. Cris Collinsworth is a very busy man who is difficult to contact. We exchanged e-mails for about six months. He'd set a day and then not be able to do it because of TV or family obligations.

As deadline approached, I was about to give up, especially when Florida's basketball run began in 2007 at the SEC Tournament in Atlanta. I was going to be the one who would be busy.

So as I settled into my press row seat to cover a game I had been looking forward to—Kentucky vs. Alabama in the first round—my cell phone rang.

"Pat, it's Cris Collinsworth."

Now?

What are you going to do? I missed the game but got the interview and Collinsworth's chapter is one of the most entertaining in the book.

Thanks for reading.

Chapter 1

CARLOS ALVAREZ

PREGAME

Alvarez was born in Havana, Cuba, where he lived until he was 10 years old, attending a private school run by Dominican Brothers.

"We were learning philosophy in first grade and they emphasized sports," he said. "Baseball was the big thing. I had no idea what a football was until I got here."

His father went to law school with Fidel Castro and knew him well enough to realize that when Castro took over it was time to leave Cuba.

"He had to convince my mom and that took him about a year," Alvarez said. "It was great living there. We were watching a revolution take place. You know how kids collect baseball cards, we used to collect bullets. The guerillas, we used to ask them for bullets. It seems bizarre now.

"We left at about the time Castro was getting ready to shut the door. We made it by a month. We took the ferry to Key West. We had visited the U.S. so we knew a little about it. The ferry brought our car over, too, and we had it packed with everything we could stuff in it. My dad was a lawyer for a shipping company and he had a lot of friends in the business. My brothers had silverware stuffed in their pockets. The authorities in

1

Havana checked each car. When they came to our car they bypassed it because my dad had paid someone off."

The family migrated to North Miami where nobody at the time spoke Spanish. At St. James Catholic School, two brothers and a sister were put into a difficult environment. The youngest Alvarez, Carlos wound up in the wrong classroom.

"I still remember the guy who sat in front of me—Paul Aaron," he said. "I did everything he did. I would put Paul Aaron on the top of my papers because he did. Because it was North Miami, I don't have an accent. Within a month I was speaking English. I have aunts who moved to South Miami who still don't speak English."

Because he played sports, it was easy to integrate himself into school. He attended North Miami High where Alvarez played running back and safety.

"I caught one pass my senior year," he said. "I had the speed and I was the second-leading rusher in Dade County. I'd have been first but in the last game, this guy named Paul Casey, they wanted him to win the rushing title and he ran for 300 yards. We played our rivals and they shut me down.

"The big thing for me was there was a Boys Club near our house, It was basketball, baseball, and football. All the kids who played basketball and baseball went out for football so I did, too."

After his junior season, Alvarez "pretty much committed" to Vanderbilt. He couldn't believe that they were offering a full ride. But during his senior year, other schools came calling.

One of them was Florida.

"Lindy Infante recruited me to Florida," he said. "He was great. He made my mother feel like he was Hispanic. Once Florida offered, they flew the family up to Gainesville. It was perfect match for me. Both of my brothers were at Florida."

Alvarez was also recruited by Miami where he had attended several games. He was a big fan of Miami quarterback George Mira, whose scrambling abilities caught Alvarez's eye.

Carlos Alvarez still owns the career record at Florida for receptions with 172. *University of Florida archives*

But when the Hurricanes were recruiting Alvarez, he found himself in coach Charley Tate's office staring at a stuffed alligator hanging from the wall.

"It was offensive to me," Alvarez said. "That's when I knew I was going to be a Gator."

Florida recruited Alvarez as a running back or a defensive back, not as a wide receiver. But at 175 pounds, he wondered if running back was the right position, especially once practice started and he saw 200-pound All-America running back Larry Smith in action.

"I thought, 'If that's the style of Florida football, I'll be dead by the end of the first year,'" he said.

Florida allowed Alvarez to try out at wide receiver. He was ready because of a strenuous workout schedule during the off-season. It was part work ethic, part fear of not making the team that drove him that summer.

"If I don't make it, I don't ever want to look back and say I should have done this or that," he said.

During the high school all-star game at Florida Field, Alvarez caught a few passes out of the backfield from John Reaves. It was a hook-up that would become Florida legend.

One of his first pass routes in practice at UF came against All-America defensive back Steve Tannen. Alvarez ran a post pattern, caught a perfect spiral from Reaves and slowed down.

"One-on-one when you have the whole field and no safety rolling over, it's not too hard," he said. "I beat Tannen clean, John threw a perfect pass, but Tannen came behind me when I stopped and just killed me.

"All of my Cuban temper came up. I jumped on him and started fighting him. The coaches were all over me, telling me you're not supposed to do that with the varsity.

"Lindy came over and said, 'Don't do that . . . but he deserved it.' After that first day, I was never going to move back."

Freshmen weren't eligible then, so Alvarez had to wait his turn. He didn't have to wait long. After lighting up the upperclassmen in pre-season practices, Reaves and Alvarez hooked up on a 70-yard touchdown pass on their first connection against Houston.

Alvarez kept it going, even making *Sports Illustrated* with his fingertip catch in a 21-6 win over Florida State. The Super Soph backfield rolled through the first six games of the season before suffering a loss at Auburn and a tie against Georgia.

Florida finished off its SEC schedule with a win over Kentucky, then had the week off before the regular-season finale against Miami.

Alvarez, for one, couldn't wait. He was going home a hero with a chance to play in front of so many people he knew.

Plus, there was a score to settle for that stuffed alligator hanging in the coach's office.

THE GAME OF MY LIFE
BY CARLOS ALVAREZ

The Miami game, from an individual standpoint, had so much going on emotionally for me. We had such a great season and to be able to go back with our team doing so well and me having a great season was special.

There are three or four games where everything is rolling right and the energy and things are flowing in the right direction and this was definitely one of them for me.

The game was in Miami on Thanksgiving weekend and it was the game I was pointing to all year. My family was pointing to it, so many friends in Miami were pointing to it. During the week I got a lot of calls from Miami people. The whole thing was channeled towards a special night.

When we got there my family was there at the hotel. I had to fly out the next day for the coaches' All-America team television appearance in New York.

I always got really tense until I got on the field. I hated night games because you have to sit there all day. You just hate it.

I had all kinds of butterflies. You have to calm yourself because you don't want to waste any energy. I meditated. Now, the kids have mp3 players, which is great. You have to keep your mind off of it or you burn out before the game.

We had a great senior class. People talk about senior leadership, well, when I think back to my sophomore year, it made things easier for the sophomores who were there. They would fire us up at the right time. Our locker room was always calm, but this was an emotional setting.

The Orange Bowl was packed and there were so many Cubans there because I was first the Cuban athlete to really play football and get some recognition. We had a lot of Gator fans and a lot of Cuban fans in the stands. Miami would usually draw 20,000, but it was packed.

Before the game, four or five of my high school friends who used to sneak into the Orange Bowl told me before the game, "Not only are we going to sneak in but we'll meet you at the 50." And there they were, not that I could do a whole lot with them, but it just cracked me up they made it that far.

You don't sneak up on anybody after that first game we had. We did sneak up on Houston, but after that a lot of times I got double-teamed, so we had to have balance.

We didn't put anything new in for this game. Our strategy was to see how the defensive backs were covering. We did the hitch just to let them know we could go long. You have to do that. It doesn't matter if you complete it or not; just get it into the defensive back's head. It opens up middle routes.

The first pass I caught was a long pattern. I figured Miami wanted to take me out of the game with double teams. On the first pass, I remember going up and catching the ball and falling even though nobody was touching me because I wanted to make sure I caught the ball.

Once I got the first one, it was all over in my mind. I knew. Even when I was warming up, I was catching everything John threw. I remember doing a 25-yard out pattern reaching out with one hand and pulling it in. It just stuck. And I was feeling the energy. My legs were fresh because we had an open date.

They single-covered me for much of the game until it started to pile up and then they doubled me. Andy Cheney was playing opposite me but he got hurt. He actually had more catches than me when he went out. John was just on.

To catch 15 passes in one game, you have to have a lot working for you. To run that many routes, you have to be fresh. It was a night game, so it wasn't hot. The other receivers have to be playing well to keep the defense from keying on you. And you have to have a close game or you're out. It was close enough although we had them the whole way. The final was 35-16.

That last catch of the game, Miami was double teaming me. Fred Pancoast, who was our offensive coordinator, put me in the slot just to get me another touchdown. I ran a fly pattern and I was wide open. They didn't have to do that for me because we had it won. I always appreciated that.

My brother Arthur came down on the field after the game. It was a magical moment.

I knew I was in double digits, but 15 catches is a lot of catches. I was truly surprised when they told me after the game.

The funny thing is we had the ball one time on the 1-yard line and I ran a fly pattern and I was 10 yards behind the defender. It was one of the few passes John didn't throw well. He underthrew it and the defender got back there and tipped it. It would have been a 99-yard touchdown.

The 15 catches is a record that still stands, although the 237 yards was broken by Taylor Jacobs in 2002. It was just a special night that I'll never forget.

THE AFTERMATH

Florida went on to win the Gator Bowl game 14-13, but Ray Graves was out as the UF coach and Doug Dickey was in. Alvarez aggravated an arthritic condition in his knee working out on the UF track during the summer and was never the same player.

"I overdid it, like I always did, just trying to get faster," he said.

He also had a problem with the way the coaching change took place and even tried to organize an athletes union.

With Dickey's run-oriented attack and his sore knees, Alvarez never had a season like 1969 as Florida went 7-4 in his junior season and 4-7 in his senior season. But he did finish with a bang, catching the final pass of the '71 season to allow Reaves to get the NCAA career passing record.

Alvarez was drafted by Dallas in the 15th round of the 1972 draft.

"They kind of surprised me," he said. "I told them I was going to law school and I'd see how it worked out, but I knew I was finished with football."

He earned a law degree at Duke, taught for four years at SMU and then worked in Jacksonville for a year.

Alvarez settled in Tallahassee where he practices law. He still makes it back to Gainesville for Gator games.

Chapter 2

NEAL ANDERSON

FLORIDA VS. KENTUCKY
NOVEMBER 13, 1982
COMMONWEALTH STADIUM
LEXINGTON, KENTUCKY

PREGAME

Anderson was born on the same day the only hospital opened in his hometown of Graceville, Florida, but the brand new hospital wasn't equipped to deliver babies. So he was actually born across the border in Dothan, Alabama, then moved to the hospital in Graceville.

There was no Boys Club in Graceville, a small town with no red light and no fast food restaurants at the time, but from the time he started playing in the playgrounds he was showing off his speed.

"I was always fast," he said. "I was the fastest in elementary school, fastest in middle school, fastest in high school. I got it from my dad. He was really fast. The old guys in town would always say, 'You're fast, but you're not as fast as your daddy.'

"When I started playing football in the seventh grade, I had three things going for me—I was fast, strong, and mean. It was a tough town, everybody working at the mill. You had to be tough to make it. So I had this mean streak, which is exactly what I needed."

At the end of his ninth grade season, Anderson was moved up to the varsity and started as a sophomore. By the time he was finished at Graceville, he had all of the school's rushing records.

"My junior and senior year, I could pretty much run for as many yards as I wanted to," he said.

But long before that, he knew where he was headed. At a recent Neal Anderson Day in Graceville, a middle school classmate showed Anderson a yearbook. Under his picture, Anderson signed it, "Neal 'Superstar' Anderson. Save this because when I'm playing pro football nobody will believe you knew me."

First he had to get to college, which was clearly not going to be a problem. Anderson dropped baseball early in high school to concentrate on football.

"My dad still thinks I made a mistake," Anderson said.

The scouts were all over Graceville. Its one hotel was constantly sold out although Anderson suspected one school was buying up all the rooms to keep the others away.

The prevailing suspicion in Graceville was that Anderson would join the long line of great tailbacks at Southern Cal, but he wanted his mother and father to be able to see him play. So it came down to three SEC schools—Alabama, Auburn, and Florida.

"I was very close to going to Alabama," he said. "When Bear Bryant came to our little town to recruit me, it was the biggest thing that had ever happened there. They let the kids out of school that day.

"I always hear the stories about guys getting rich off recruiting. Heck, my family went into debt. Every time a Bear Bryant or a Pat Dye was coming to my living room, we'd go out and buy stuff to make it look good."

Bryant told Anderson that the Tide was ditching the Wishbone offense and going to the power-I formation which featured the tailback. He didn't believe the old coach. Why would he make the change? It didn't make sense. As it turns out, Alabama did just that the following year.

"The hardest thing I had to do was call Coach Bryant and tell him I wasn't coming," Anderson said. "He was so nice to me. When the word got out, there was this booster who came over to my house and walked right in and turned our TV off. Right in our house. You should have seen the look on my mother's face."

Neal Anderson was named second-team All-SEC in 1984 and first team the following year as a senior. *University of Florida archives*

In the end, his decision came down to this—if you go to Alabama and win, so what? The Tide had a long history of championships. You're just another one of those guys who got it done in Tuscaloosa.

If you go to Florida, which had never won the SEC, and win big, it could be something special.

To the people back in Graceville, it didn't make any sense. The town was still buzzing from the whole recruiting process that had been a circus with college football royalty walking the streets daily. That was exciting, but the decision was puzzling.

Florida already had James Jones and Lorenzo Hampton in the backfield and had signed another big-time running back in John L. Williams. Why would Neal want to go to a crowded house?

"Everyone thought I was crazy," Anderson said. "But I knew I could play at that level. I was very confident. People were wondering how I was going to handle the big city which Gainesville was compared to Graceville. But I wasn't worried."

Neal Superstar Anderson was heading for college with pro aspirations. But it wouldn't be easy to crack a line-up that had so much talent.

It's amazing that an 8-4 season would be chronicled so often in these pages—this is one of four games from 1982 chosen by the players who were picked for this book—but the '82 season was a wild ride.

As the season began, Anderson was at the bottom of the depth chart. In addition to Williams, Hampton, and Jones, Florida had signed Joe Henderson and Leon Pennington. The good news for Anderson was that Charley Pell was drifting away from the one-back sets that Mike Shanahan had brought to Gainesville, using the fullback more.

Still, the fiesty Anderson saw it another way.

"I always thought it was political," he said. "There were no boosters in my hometown. Actually there was one doctor who gave a little bit of money. I thought that made a difference.

"But when we'd be out on the practice field, they had trouble tackling me. I was getting very frustrated that I wasn't playing."

Florida opened with dramatic wins over Miami and Southern Cal, but three SEC losses doomed UF's chances of a conference title again. A 44-0 loss to Georgia was especially humiliating.

Next up—Kentucky in Lexington. Back then, Florida always played the Wildcats in November when the grass had turned brown and cold was in the air. The boys from the Sunshine State often had a difficult time with the Wildcats.

THE GAME OF MY LIFE
BY NEAL ANDERSON

Up to this point, I was hardly playing at all. I was frustrated and upset and wondering why they wouldn't let me get in there. I knew I could play. I knew I could do something big. I also knew that this week would be my chance.

Lorenzo Hampton got into trouble with some kind of phone issue and was suspended. John L. Williams pulled a hamstring in practice a couple of days before the game. Leon Pennington had moved to linebacker. They had to play me now. I was the only tailback left.

Vince Kendrick was the running backs coach and he came to me to tell me that Coach Pell had decided to go with the one-back set for this game and just use James Jones. I couldn't believe it. Why did they think I couldn't play at this level? I knew I could.

So I went to Mickey Andrews, who was a defensive coach but had recruited me to Florida. He covered the Panhandle for them. I told him that I appreciated everything he had done for me, but that this was going to be it for me at Florida. I was breaking tackles in practice, I had the speed, I knew what I was doing and they were down to one tailback and I wasn't going to play. I was going home.

The day before the game, Vince came to me and told me I was starting. I guess they believed I was going to quit and they didn't want me to leave.

The night before the game, I slept like a baby. I always did, especially when I knew I wasn't going to play. There was usually no adrenaline rush when I'd put the uniform on. But it was there for this game. There was a lot of excitement.

I knew I could do it, but you never know what is going to happen in one given game. Is the line going to block well for you? And I knew that if I didn't have a good game, it might be a long time before I got another chance. I knew I needed to make something happen, but sometimes when you think like that you press and make mistakes. So I had to try to be calm but there was a lot of excitement running through me.

James Jones helped me stay calm. He kept patting me on the head. And right before the game, he came over and hit me pretty hard. I hit him back. He was trying to get me ready. We kept hitting each other, harder and harder. The adrenaline was definitely flowing.

Our plan was to run the ball against them. I don't know if they were keying on someone else, but I kept getting yards. I'd get five and then 10. It was a snowball effect. Once we got rolling, they couldn't stop us.

We beat them pretty easily, 39-13, and the yards kept piling up. But I had no idea how many I had. Back in those days, there was nobody on the sideline to tell you how many yards you had. Today, if a guy is getting close to 100 or breaking a record, there's somebody there to tell the coach.

So I just kept running, ripping off yards. James was genuinely excited. He kept slapping me on the helmet after every run, really hard, keeping me going.

At the end of the game, I was hoping I had 100 yards. But I had no idea how many I had. In the locker room, the reporters came to me and told me I had rushed for 197 yards. I was surprised. At the time, it was the fourth highest total for any Gator running back in history.

I carried the ball 33 times, which was the most ever for a Florida player. But I wasn't tired. I just kept running.

It's funny because I didn't keep many game balls or trophies during my career. When I'd get a game ball with the Bears, I'd come out of the locker and there would be a bunch of kids and I'd play with them and give one of them the game ball. But the one game ball that is still in my father's house is the one from that game. That was a special one.

The big thing was that I knew I could play like that and now I had shown the coaches I could. I had my big chance and I capitalized on it. It was a special feeling. And I remember Coach Andrews and his wife were real excited. He had talked to me about playing defensive back because I liked to hit people. A lot of schools recruited me as a defensive back. But there was no question where I was going to play after that game.

THE AFTERMATH

Anderson remained in the starting line-up for the remainder of his career. Over the next three years, he led the team in rushing. In 1984,

Florida got that first SEC championship, only to have it stripped that summer by the conference presidents because of NCAA violations.

In 1985, Anderson was a first-round pick by the Chicago Bears. Walter Payton was entering the last years of his career, and the Bears wanted to groom a replacement.

"It was difficult for him," Anderson said. "I wanted to play. The first year, I told Mike Ditka if I didn't play I was going to quit. He put me on special teams. I was supposed to play safety but I'd see a hole and barrel through it to get the return man. So he just told me to go find the ball.

"The next year they put me at fullback, but they ran a lot of tailback plays for me. That was it for Walter. He retired the next year."

Although Ditka and Anderson often butted heads, Anderson was the only NFL back to go over 1,000 yards in each of the 1988, 1989, and 1990 seasons. He made four straight Pro Bowls, rushing for 6,166 career yards and scoring 71 touchdowns rushing and receiving before retiring after the 1993 season.

Anderson returned to Gainesville where he has taken the money he earned in pro football and turned it into thriving businesses. He owns a peanut farm in Williston and is part-owner of seven banks in the area. Most of his time is spent shuttling his three children—T.C., Camille, and Brianna—to their sporting events.

Chapter 3

JAMES BATES

PREGAME

Although his father played at Tennessee and his mom went to school there, James Bates didn't move to the state until his high school freshman year. Until then, he had been bouncing around the country as his father Jim moved for coaching jobs.

"We always watched the Vols," Bates said. "It was Daddy's team. I always had Tennessee stuff. But we were always on the move. I think that's one of the things that helped me adjust later in life, to be able to adapt to so many different people. We'd be somewhere a couple of years and start wondering when we were going to move again."

His parents divorced when Bates was 12 and his mother moved to New York. He spent time with both parents, but when his father got a job as an assistant at Tennessee, both sides agreed to move there for some stability for James and his younger brother Jeremy.

Bates went to Bearden High in Knoxville, but the coach at Seiver County High (Mike Biddix) wanted him to come to the school 20 miles away in Seiverville.

"My mom was looking for a job so I told him that if he got her a job I'd come," Bates said. "He did, but when we got there, of course, there was no job."

Bates had shown off his talent as a freshman playing for the varsity in Rochester, New York, a 185-pound wide receiver and outside linebacker with a nose for the ball. He fit right in at Seiver County (nicknamed the Smoky Bears) and enjoyed both school and sports.

As a sophomore he played some strong safety before moving to inside linebacker. As a junior, he played one of his best games in a playoff loss to Todd Helton's Knox County team, turning on recruiters for the following season.

"We didn't make the playoffs my senior season," he said. "One of my biggest regrets was that we didn't finish up well."

A high school All-American playing just outside of the Tennessee campus where his dad had been a player and a coach? Well, he's just got to go play for the Vols.

"Tennessee football was all they had up there," Bates said. "My dream was to play big-time college football. There was a feeling then that if you were being recruited by Tennessee, why would you want to go anywhere else?

"But it was a little too close to home. I was ready for something new. I was used to moving every couple of years so I was getting a little antsy. And a big thing for me was that I had to wear No. 44. I was a big Brian Bosworth fan when I was living in Texas. Fee Bartley had just graduated from Florida and that was his number.

"And Florida was sexy. Coach (Steve) Spurrier, I'll never forget him telling me this, 'All of the people up where you are want to turn 60 so they can come down to Florida and live.' That stuck with me."

Little did he know that was the same pitch that had been presented to Spurrier when he left East Tennessee for Gainesville.

Jim Bates wanted his son to make his own decision. Joyce Bates was a heavy Tennessee lean. Bates made trips to UCLA, Michigan, Texas, Tennessee and Florida. The only one that included his mother was Tennessee.

But as soon as he visited Florida, he knew where he wanted to be.

James Bates (44) was one of the best players on Florida's 1996 national title team and has parlayed his personality into a television career.
The Gainesville Sun

"I was in Coach Spurrier's office and he said we should call Mom and Dad," he said. "Mom said, 'That's nice. I'll see you when you get home.' Then she hung up. I pretended like I was still talking to her.

"It was bad in the Bates house for a while. Coach Spurrier and Coach (Jim) Collins came up a few weeks later and told her how happy they were that I was going to be a Gator. She said, 'If it were up to me you wouldn't be sitting in this house.' But the day I left was the day she went and got all of her Florida gear."

After he signed with UF, Bates wore a shirt to every workout in Seiverville.

It read, in magic marker, "9/17."

The date of Florida's game that year in Knoxville.

"I just wanted to be part of that rivalry," he said. "I wanted to help them lose to Florida, to make 100,000 people go home crying."

It didn't work out the first year. Bates was injured and didn't dress, but he did make the trip as the Vols won easily on a rainy day.

"It was a terrible experience," he said. "I was soaked and that was the flight where we lost cabin pressure. We were joking that the headline would say, 'Gators Get Killed Twice.' I just knew I never wanted a repeat of that day."

Florida won in Gainesville the following season and again in Knoxville 31-0 in 1994. In 1995, the Gators trailed 30-14 before storming back to win 62-37.

"My brother was playing for the Vols and he got in late," Bates said. "I went charging back in so I could give him a pop, but all he did was hand off."

Florida finished the '95 season with a devastating loss to Nebraska in the national title game, but there was plenty of optimism for 1996. Danny Wuerffel was back at quarterback, the skill positions were set and the defense returned a talented group.

There was only one thing on the minds of the players.

Tennessee.

"We had beaten them three straight times and that was all we thought about all summer," Bates said. "Peyton Manning was the big thing, they had just expanded their stadium and they were saying up there that this was the year they were going to get the Gators.

"It was going to be a clash of the titans. It's what we worked for all summer. The days just dragged on. We knew that in '95 we made it to the show and totally blew it. What are the chances to get back? So many things have to fall into place. One little slip-up. But we knew we had to beat Tennessee if we were going to win the East."

Florida opened the season with easy wins over Southwestern Louisiana and Georgia Southern. The week was here. No. 2 Tennessee vs. No. 4 Florida.

THE GAME OF MY LIFE
BY JAMES BATES

I remember, as a senior, feeling that this was our chance to make another run at it. A lot of things would have to happen for us to get to the title game, but it started with this game. On top of that, I was going home for the last time to play in front of all of those Tennessee fans, I was just so happy to be a part of that rivalry.

That's what made it so great to go to a place like Tennessee, that their fans were so good and they all hated you. You had a chance to shut them all up. Now, here we were with a chance to do it in my senior year and make it four in a row.

It was everything. I feel almost guilty that I got to be a part of that game.

It was like two nations that hate each other the way those fans hate each other.

During the week, a couple of our players made some comments that were turned into a big deal. They were talking about how Peyton has happy feet. You never want to give anyone any extra ammunition, but a game like this is past the point of pumping it up anymore. Spurrier knew that, too, so he didn't make a big deal about it around the team.

It's funny, because when I was playing we owned Georgia, but it was different with Tennessee. There was more respect for them because you knew you were going to have to play at a certain level to beat them.

Riding into the game, I always enjoyed it in Knoxville because East Tennessee is beautiful. And then you see the Vol Nation and the Vol Navy and you can't help but be ready to play. To think that all of these people want you to fail, it motivates you.

We got to the locker room and it was a locker room I had been around a lot from the days when my dad was a coach there. It was raining and you just tried to settle down and concentrate on what you had to do.

But the excitement for that game was unbelievable because you had this great rivalry and the newly expanded stadium and a showdown of Heisman Trophy candidates, and I mean there was nothing this game didn't have.

So we got the ball first and we drove it down there and got stopped. It was 4th-and-11 on their 35 and Spurrier was going for it. I remember thinking that I was glad to be on the same sideline with Steve Spurrier. And Reidel Anthony got behind the defense for a touchdown. We were going crazy on the sideline, and the fans from Tennessee were just blown away.

It was the defense's turn, and Teako Brown picked off a Manning pass and we scored again. And then in the second quarter, I came in on a blitz and did what they always taught me, to make sure I got my hands up. I tipped the ball and it hit Ed Chester in the knee and came right back to me. Peyton must have been thinking, "I can't do anything."

It was perfect for me. It was storybook. I was in my last game in Tennessee and I was making a bunch of tackles and then I got the interception. People were screaming, "We hate you, Bates." I was loving every minute of it.

After my interception, Danny threw another touchdown pass and we were up 28-0. They ran a sweep and fumbled right to Anthone Lott and he ran it in for a touchdown. It was 35-0 and we had only played 20 minutes.

We might have lost a little intensity after that because they came back and scored 29 points, but we never felt like we were going to lose the game. The great thing was that they had made such a big deal about the additional seats, and so many people were leaving at halftime.

After the game, a reporter asked me what I thought about all of the people leaving so early. I told him, "I don't know why they left. Maybe *The Jeff Foxworthy Show* was on." That got a lot of laughs from Gator fans.

THE AFTERMATH

Even though the victory was huge, the Gator players knew it was simply one step.

"It was so early in the season," Bates said. "We knew we had a lot of work to do to get back to the title game."

Focused and talented, Florida steamrolled its opposition before losing the regular-season finale against Florida State. After winning against Alabama in the SEC title game, the Gators caught a break when Ohio State beat unbeaten Arizona State in the Rose Bowl.

That meant a showdown with FSU for the national title in the Sugar Bowl. The Gators won 52-20, but Bates missed the second half after suffering a concussion in a collision with Clarence "Pooh Bear" Williams, the Seminoles' massive fullback.

Bates made a stab at the NFL, trying out for Dallas and making the practice squad, but he soon returned to Gainesville.

Bates is married, and he and his wife, Tina, have three children. They moved from Gainesville to Colorado in 2006 when Bates was named the head play-by-play man for the Mountain West Sports Network.

He continues to work towards getting *The James Bates Show*, his offbeat look at the world of sports, on a network.

Chapter 4

KERWIN BELL

PREGAME

Growing up the son of tobacco farmer in tiny Mayo, Florida, Kerwin Bell gravitated to sports. He played football, basketball, and baseball for Lafayette High, leading that team to the playoffs for the first time ever in 1981 when he was a junior. That team won the state championship running the veer option, but Bell often dropped back out of the veer to fling passes down the field.

But in the early 1980s, scouts weren't flocking to Mayo.

"We didn't have any highlight tapes to send out back then, and scouting wasn't as sophisticated," he said. "Nobody from Lafayette had ever signed a Div. 1 scholarship in any sport."

Only one scout ventured to Mayo to look at Bell, a defensive coach from Div. 1-AA Valdosta State. He liked what he saw and told Bell he thought he could play at a higher level, but if Florida and Florida State didn't offer, Valdosta State was ready to give him a scholarship.

But that coach was talked out of it by Valdosta head coach Jim Goodman.

25

"Later on, I was a grad assistant at Florida and Jim Goodman was the recruiting coordinator with the Gators," Bell said. "I told him, 'I thank God you didn't offer me a scholarship.' He had turned me down."

Bell was a Florida State fan in middle school during the Seminoles' rise to power, but that changed when he started dating his current wife, Cosette. Her father was a huge Gator fan and he began attending Florida games with the family.

When it came time to choose a college, he had an interesting dilemma. Florida was loaded at quarterback and FSU was not. The Gators had given out three scholarships that year to quarterbacks Scott Rismiller, Pat Pinner, and Derrick Crudup.

"But it's like I was telling one of the players when I was coaching in high school (Trinity Catholic in Belleview where Bell was the head coach)," he said. "I told him he'd know in his heart when it was the right school. You have to go where you want to be for the next five years even if you don't end up playing football. Where do you want to have your degree from? Florida is where I wanted to be even if I didn't play a down."

So Bell walked on at Florida and soon was hit with a dose of reality. As he walked out of the locker room in the south end zone for the first practice, the depth chart was posted on the wall.

There were eight quarterbacks listed. He was No. 8.

"All I really did was help out where I was needed," he said. "Helping out with the scout team. I remember Joe Kines was our defensive coordinator and he was working on the proper drops for the linebackers. He wanted the receivers to run in-routes and for me to throw it right to the hash where the linebacker was waiting.

"I got tired of that after a while so I waited until the receiver cleared and then threw it to him and completed it. Coach Kines said, 'Bell, if you do that again I'll break your arm.'"

The one day of the week that was fun for Bell was Monday when the Gators would have *Monday Night Football*, allowing the scrubs to play against each other.

"I was really able to show what I could do," he said. "Coach (Mike) Shanahan told me, 'You're going to be the guy one day.'"

But while Shanahan left for Denver after the 1983 season, so did three players ahead of Bell on the depth chart. Still, he was fifth-string and Florida planned to work with only four quarterbacks.

When Kerwin Bell got married to Cosette Odom, it was one of the biggest events in Mayo, Florida. *The Gainesville Sun*

Bell was told before the Orange and Blue game he'd get one series and he took advantage of it, driving his team to a touchdown while completing all three of his passes and running for 15 yards. After the spring game, Charley Pell told Bell, "You're a darkhorse candidate."

By now, Goodman and Valdosta State wanted Bell, but he decided to stick with Florida. Little did he know what was about to happen.

First, sophomore quarterback Donnie Whiting failed out of school, meaning Bell was in the top four for summer drills. Pell and new offensive coordinator Galen Hall graded each quarterback on every practice. On the Monday before the opener against Miami, Pell told the team that Dale Dorminey was No. 1 and Bell was his back-up.

The next day during a goal-line drill, Dorminey was running an option play when a fullback was blocked into the quarterback's leg.

Ricky Nattiel, a sophomore receiver, walked up to Bell and told him, "Country, you have to grow up in a hurry."

That night in the dining hall, it became official.

"Galen walked up to me while I was in line and told me I was starting," Bell said. "I was scared to death. I couldn't eat. I went up to the offices and started watching film and praying a lot."

Bell nearly led Florida to an upset win over Miami in Tampa in his first game. Florida was 1-1-1 under Bell when Pell was ousted as the Florida coach and Hall was named interim.

It was a shock to the team, which was battered by daily questions about NCAA violations.

"I think it pulled us together," Bell said.

The Gators won the rest of their games that season and captured the school's first SEC title. But the following spring, the league stripped Florida of the crown because of the NCAA violations committed under Pell's rule.

"We still have the rings," Bell said. "Everyone knows who won it."

In January of 1985, Bell was given a scholarship and by then had a nickname—the Throwin' Mayoan. The following year, the Gators won nine games again. But by 1986, the scholarship limitations had begun to take their toll on Florida.

Florida began the 1986 season with high expectations because of Bell, Nattiel, and a strong defense. The Gators were ranked 13th in the preseason polls and opened with an easy win over Georgia Southern.

But then, everything went sour.

Florida lost four in a row to Miami, Alabama, Mississippi State, and LSU. In the LSU loss, Bell suffered an injury, tearing the meniscus in his left knee.

He was told by Dr. Pete Indelicato that he was out for the year. Bell told him he'd be back for Auburn.

"Nobody really believed me," Bell said.

He had four weeks to let it heal as UF had easy games against Vanderbilt and New Mexico followed by an open date. Rodney Brewer would be the quarterback.

"They let me practice the week of the Auburn game, but it was killing me," Bell said. "I had a big brace on and I wasn't moving too well. Galen told me he'd dress me, but he wasn't going to let me play unless there was an emergency. I just wanted to play."

THE GAME OF MY LIFE
BY KERWIN BELL

Auburn came in ranked fifth in the nation with a ferocious defense led by Aundray Bruce and Tracy Rocker. They were killing us. It wasn't Rodney's fault, there was just so much pressure and he kept fumbling and throwing interceptions.

We had a back-up quarterback named Pepe Lezcano and he came over to me in the second quarter and said, "Kerwin, I think you're going into the game." I was thinking that I didn't know if I wanted to. Standing on the sidelines, it was kind of scary.

Our defense was saving us because we gave them the ball on our side of the field something like five times and it was only 14-0. They put me in at the end of the first half and we didn't do anything. But we got the ball back and moved it a little and I started feeling better.

It was 17-0 late in the third quarter and we started a drive that we finished in the fourth quarter. I snuck it in for a touchdown and it was 17-7. But I felt terrible. I couldn't even drop back, I was throwing off my back foot. It was unbelievable how I was getting it done.

We stopped them and got the ball back and had a little drive. And then Robert McGinty kicked a 51-yard field goal. Then it was 17-10 and that gave us a chance. We felt like we had the momentum.

But they went on a drive. They kept giving it to Brent Fullwood and got it down to our 40. They gave it to their fullback on a belly play and he fumbled; we recovered with just a couple of minutes to play.

On the first play, they sacked me, but they grabbed my facemask. That gave us new life.

I was basically playing on instinct. On one play, they spun me by my shirt but just before I went into a full spin I saw a running back out there and when I came back around I just threw it where I knew he was for a completion.

There was a play where I threw a pass out in front of Ricky Nattiel and the defensive back drove him into the ground, separating his shoulder. He went out of the game, and Dr. Pete told him he was done. But later in the drive he snuck out on the field.

I threw him a corner route and somehow he got both arms stretched out to catch it. He had to be in unbelievable pain.

So we were down around the five and called a play where Ricky runs a fade from the inside. They had a kid on him who couldn't run with him. I took my steps and saw the corner didn't switch, so I just threw it out there for Ricky for the touchdown.

As soon as we scored, we called timeout. They wanted us to go for two. I said, "What?" I was ready to tie it up. But we started thinking about plays and we came up with an option route for Ricky.

I drifted to his side but they were doubling him. We had nothing. I felt pressure from my right side and stepped to the left. David Williams saw me start forward and made an unbelievable block for me. I knew I had it. I also knew I was going to get hit so I made sure I went low.

Once I scored to give us the 18-17 win, I just raised up and tossed the ball in the air. But Bob Sims, our offensive guard, landed on me and bent me back. He didn't hurt my left knee but I have had tendinitis in my right one ever since.

I was so exhausted when it was over. I hadn't been running for four weeks and I was out of football shape. My legs were gone.

The other day, I was at lunch and someone came over and said something about the Auburn game. My former quarterback, Johnny Brantley, asked his dad, "Did Kerwin ever play against anybody but Auburn?"

THE AFTERMATH

The next week, Florida beat 19th-ranked Georgia in Jacksonville with the sore-shouldered Nattiel catching three touchdown passes from Bell. They closed the season by beating Florida State—the Bell-to-Nattiel combination resulting in the winning score—to finish 6-5 after a 1-4 start.

In 1987, Emmitt Smith would show up along with one of the best recruiting classes in Florida history. But NCAA sanctions had decimated the program and Bell was often running for his life.

"We were two-deep at every position in '84 and '85," he said. "But by 1987, we had guys starting who shouldn't have even been playing."

Despite a sensational freshman season from Smith, Florida again went 6-5 before losing to UCLA in the Aloha Bowl.

Because of his injuries, Bell lasted until the seventh round of the draft before Miami picked him. He bounced around several NFL teams and had a successful CFL career before turning to coaching.

Bell got a head coaching job at a newly formed school—Trinity Catholic—and used a combination of what he learned from Lindy Infante when he was at Indianapolis and Steve Spurrier when Bell was a grad assistant at UF to create a hybrid offense that was good enough to win the state championship in 2005.

After the 2006 season, Bell was named the new head coach at Div. 1-AA Jacksonville University where he hopes to turn around that program.

Chapter 5

SCOT BRANTLEY

PREGAME

Scot Brantley was born in Chester, South Carolina, a small town near Spartanburg and lived there for eight years before moving to Greenville, South Carolina. His father was a bridge contractor who built bridges all over the Southeast.

When the state of Florida decided to build the Cross Florida Barge Canal, an ill-fated idea that was never completed, Brantley's father decided to move the family to Ocala where his plan was to build bridges in the Ocala National Forest.

"He came down here and fell in love with Ocala," Brantley said.

In South Carolina, Scot and his older brother John played in textile leagues where tackle football in full gear was the norm for eight-year-old boys. But when the family moved to Ocala, they found no organized tackle football for kids.

The Brantleys spent a couple of months passing the hat to collect money to start a league. At the time, youngsters in Marion County had to wait until high school to play football, but the arrival of the Brantleys also meant the arrival of youth football to Ocala.

"The first two years of it, those were the two classes who went on to Ocala Forest and won back-to-back state championships," Brantley said. "People understood after that that the idea of having midget football might be a good idea.

"John always played quarterback, and I was a linebacker and a fullback. We were extremely close. It was a great advantage to have a brother who was only 11 months older than I was. It was like we were twins. I'd tell my momma, if she knew anything about family planning, I wouldn't have been born so close to Johnny. I asked her, 'I was a mistake wasn't I?' She said, 'No, you were a pleasant surprise.'

"We fought every day, competed. I think that's what made us what we are today. We're best friends but back then we were at each other's throats."

It was as an eighth grader that Brantley first began to catch the eyes of the varsity coaches. The varsity practiced on one field and the kids on another one down the hill from the varsity.

"Every afternoon, coach Brett Hall would walk under the oak tree up on the practice field and watch and ask, 'Who's that kid? We need to find out,'" Brantley said.

By the time he became a freshman at Forest, the school had changed from the junior high system and he was allowed to play varsity football. Not only play, but start.

Ocala Forest suddenly became a power in state high school football. At one point, Brantley's team recorded six straight shutouts to jump into the top 10 in the high school rankings. In 1974 and '75, Forest won the state championship.

"We lost one game in two years, and in that game I had the best game of my life," Brantley said. "I had 36 tackles. I mean, I made every tackle in that game, but we lost to Leesburg 6-0."

The letters started coming in his sophomore year. Ocala was and is a big Gator town only 30 miles from Gainesville, and Brantley was always leaning toward the Gators.

But when Bear Bryant and Woody Hayes visit your home, you tend to listen.

Scott Brantley's brother played at Florida and his nephew Johnny is also a quarterback at UF. *University of Florida archives*

"Nobody from my county ever had a chance to play for coaches like that," Brantley said. "And being selfish, I just wanted to visit as many schools as possible and enjoy the trips, see what the schools were like. I had a good time but I wasn't serious about most of the other schools."

Those visits included trips to Georgia and Tennessee, but in the end it came down to Florida and Alabama. John Brantley had already set up shop at Florida and Scot had visited him there numerous times.

But the Bear was persistent.

"I remember Bear Bryant calling me every Wednesday night for a year and a half," Brantley said. "You could put your hand on the phone and it would ring at 6 p.m. every Wednesday night. He'd talk for five or 10 minutes, but it was hardly anything about football.

"Curley Hallman was recruiting me for Alabama and he and I would go fishing or hunting every time he came down. We really hit it off. I still have a picture Coach Bryant sent me. It said, 'We're counting on you at 'Bama.'"

Still, the allure of playing a half-hour away with his brother was too much. So was the attraction that has been a key for so many Gator recruits. Brantley knew he wanted to live in Florida after he was through with football. So why leave?

But telling Bryant that he was going to Florida wasn't easy.

Hallman told Brantley there was no way the coach was going to deliver that news to the legend. He made Brantley make the call.

"Curley told me, 'I'm not calling him. You tell him,'" Brantley said. "I cried when I talked to him.

"He lied to me though. He said he could almost guarantee that Alabama was going to win a national championship while I was there. He lied. They won two. But I didn't regret coming to Florida for one minute."

As a freshman in camp in 1976, Brantley wasn't even listed on the depth chart because there were so many players on the roster. But he liked the coaching staff, people like Doug Knotts, Jimmy Dunn, Allen Trammell, and Kim Helton, and was at the place he wanted to be.

Florida opened the season with North Carolina in Tampa, and both of the Brantleys were thrilled just to be dressed out.

"Me and Johnny were down there in our uniforms, night game, and we're just thinking this is cool," Brantley said. "I hadn't even been paying attention in the linebacker meetings. I didn't know any of the signals. There was no way I was going to play.

"And all of a sudden, they're calling my name. 'Brantley, get in for (Kevin) Logan!' I'm like, 'Go in for who? Me?' I ran out there and looked over at the sideline and I had no idea what they were calling. I asked Scott Hutchinson, who was a defensive tackle, what play they were calling."

Brantley started the second half of that game and never came out of another game until an injury in his senior season. That was a different game, when there was no situational substituting or nickel packages.

Brantley just played.

"Football is overblown," he said. "There are no geniuses in football. It's football—11 on 11. You just line up and play. It's not brain surgery. It's such a simple game. It's 90 percent emotion.

"That's the thing, I played baseball for the fun of it and to get out of spring football practice. I got drafted in the third round by the Mets out of high school. But baseball was just fun. I played football because that's what I do."

Florida lost that game in Tampa, 24-21 to North Carolina. It was a disappointing start to the season, but it was the beginning of a stellar career at UF for Brantley.

He started the next game at home in a 49-14 win over Houston. But he also knew that everything would change the next week.

"My first SEC game and it being at home, I was excited about this one," he said.

Mississippi State would be coming to Gainesville with an explosive offense. Neither team was ranked, but that never matters in the SEC.

THE GAME OF MY LIFE
BY SCOT BRANTLEY

You know, from the time I was five years old, my only fear was that I wasn't going to be big enough to play at the next level. I knew that if I was, I was going to be playing in the NFL. Just knew it.

I had a genuine belief. I was totally convinced about my future. I knew I was going to a major university and play in the NFL. I just knew it.

So even though I was surprised when I went in to play my first game, it was pretty much business as usual to be playing from then on. I had a lot of big games, but the one that stands out was that first SEC game because this was why I came to Florida, for those conference games.

I knew everything was going to be different from our first two games even though the Houston game was my first home game because this was the SEC. And at the time, playing against Mississippi State was a big deal.

They had a great offense with Walter Packer at tailback and Bruce Threadgill at quarterback. Our offense was pretty good, too, so we knew it was going to be high-scoring. The key was going to be making the big stop when you had to make it.

Running out of that tunnel was just invigorating and then seeing the Bulldogs in their maroon and white. I mean, you were just ready to play some football.

And knowing that everybody in the stands was rooting for you. I felt like I knew everybody at the game. This was my support staff and I wasn't going to let them down.

I never came out of the game and it was hot as hell on that artificial surface. We didn't have a nickel package or a dime package. There were no situational substitutions. You just played. And as the game went on and they started coming back on us, you really had to suck it up. But you played on adrenaline. I never really felt tired. I was just flying around.

They ran the same kind of stuff you see a lot of teams running today. They ran the option out of a broken wishbone and you had to be on your toes for all kinds of misdirection.

I had an interception and something like 15 tackles, which is what I averaged that year. We had a comfortable lead but they came back to cut it to 34-30 and they had the ball last. I knew it was going to come down to making one big play.

We were in a bit of a prevent defense on the last play of the game. They threw an underneath route to Packer, hoping he could make one guy miss and take it to the end zone. He was an excellent player on a very good team.

I just set myself and watched his hips. He made a couple of juke moves, but I didn't flinch. I brought him down and that was it, the game was over.

It was a great feeling to have played so well in my first SEC game.

I was in class on Monday and someone came up to me and told me I was the SEC defensive player of the week. As a freshman. They had read it in the paper.

It's the game I'll never forget for that reason. To have this belief that you can play at a certain level and then to go out and do it and be SEC defensive player of the week in your third game, man, that was a feeling that was something special.

THE AFTERMATH

Brantley went on to start every game that season as well as his sophomore and junior seasons.

But in the second game of his senior season, Brantley's helmet collided with a Georgia Tech running back's knee. The blow was so severe it caused a bruise on Brantley's brain and knocked him unconscious.

"I figured it was just going to get me out of practice," he said. "The knee had gone through the helmet and padding and scalp and skull and put a bruise on my left frontal lobe. The neurologist looked at it and told me I'd have to miss a game or two."

Brantley was floored, but there was worse news on the horizon. He was called into Pell's office where his family was waiting.

"They all looked like they had seen a ghost," he said. "Coach Pell said I was finished, that I'd never play football again. I never really got an explanation why.

"But I knew that if I ever got a second chance I would make the most of it. I had a whole different outlook. I used to hate practice but when I came back I couldn't wait for it."

Brantley flew to Dallas where the Cowboys wanted him to see a neurologist. He then went to Johns Hopkins for another look.

"I'll never forget the doctor saying, 'You missed your senior year because of this? I'd be pissed off.' Flying back, it was like a weight had been lifted off my shoulders."

Brantley expected to be drafted by the Cowboys, watching the draft at his brother's house, when a woman named Judy Kane called from the office of the Tampa Bay Bucs and said, "We just drafted you."

He played eight seasons for Tampa Bay, where he recorded 622 tackles and was voted one of the top 50 Buccaneers of all time by *Buccaneer Magazine*.

Brantley stayed in Tampa after retiring and worked for years as the Bucs color analyst as well as Florida's. Today he still works for the Gator

Radio Network and hosts a sports talk show in Tampa. His No. 55 was retired by Florida, but Steve Spurrier took both Brantley's number and his own No. 11 out of retirement when Spurrier became the coach at UF.

Chapter 6

NOAH BRINDISE AND DOUG JOHNSON

PREGAME

Coming out of Cypress Lakes in Fort Myers, there weren't a lot of scholarships being offered to Brindise. He settled on a partial scholarship to Wingate, injured his shoulder during two-a-days, and redshirted.

"My best friend signed with Purdue and they were playing at North Carolina State so I went to see him," he said. "That was what I wanted, that kind of atmosphere."

Brindise had been in touch with Florida receivers coach Dwayne Dixon and decided to try out at Florida.

"I was flying under the radar," he said. "I didn't meet Coach (Steve) Spurrier until the first day of spring practice. I was a scout team quarterback with Brian Schottenheimer. I was just fired up that I had made the team."

In 1995, Brindise was the fourth-team quarterback, played in two games, and threw three passes. The following year, he thought he would be the back-up, but Johnson arrived fresh from a summer of playing minor league baseball.

"Doug came in and Coach got enamored with him," he said. "I played in four or five games but Doug always went in before me. It was kind of disappointing."

Florida won the national title in 1996 setting up a battle between Johnson and Brindise in 1997. But Johnson had an excellent spring game and was named the starter.

"I was kind of expecting it," Brindise said. "Jesse Palmer was there, too, but he didn't have a real good spring."

Johnson got off to a terrific start before the Gators lost at LSU. Early the next week, Spurrier discovered that Johnson had missed a Thursday curfew and suspended him for the Auburn game. Palmer, a true freshman, was named the starter.

"I kind of knew he wasn't going to play well," Brindise said. "He wasn't ready. I was ready for that one."

Brindise came into the game and led Florida to a 24-10 win. Against Georgia, Spurrier tried all three quarterbacks but none of them were successful in the first loss by a Spurrier-coached team to the Bulldogs.

"He always said he never should have taken me out of the game," Brindise said.

Doug Johnson was a three-sports star from the time he was old enough to show up at the Boys Club. Baseball was actually his best sport and he didn't even start playing offense on the football team until eighth grade.

"I'll be honest, I didn't even keep up with Florida football," he said. "I wasn't a big college fan. I was into the pro sports and liked the Redskins and Cardinals. Maybe it was just that college football was so close to me it didn't excite me."

He took over the starting quarterback job at Buchholz as a sophomore and was heavily recruited, but Johnson was also being pulled out of class as a senior to work out for professional baseball teams.

He told them all the same thing—don't draft me if you think I'm not playing football.

Noah Brindise (left) and Doug Johnson (right) shared quarterback duties in 1997 with Jesse Palmer. *The Gainesville Sun*

"Playing quarterback is the toughest job in any sport," he said. "It's so demanding. It's like that girl you can't have but you keep pursuing her harder. That's what football was for me."

Johnson dropped to the second round of the baseball draft because he had signed to play football at Florida.

"It made too much sense to sign with Florida," he said. "I visited Miami, Florida State. I talked to Tennnesee, and I was going to go visit because it looked like Coach (Steve) Spurrier was going to go to the NFL. He called me out of class to tell me he wasn't going anywhere and not to take that trip."

Johnson played with the Tampa Bay Devil Rays rookie league team before his freshman season and was the third-team quarterback on the national champions. He played minor league baseball in West Virginia the following summer but had little trouble winning the job for the '97 season.

Florida started fast before the loss to LSU, and Johnson was suspended for missing a Thursday curfew.

"There was never, ever a Thursday curfew," Johnson said. "But the stuff had hit the fan and someone wanted some answers. I was the only one who stepped up. I don't lie.

"Looking back, it was the good thing that it happened. It made me stronger. Weak-minded people can't play football. You have to be strong mentally."

Johnson never really found his touch the rest of the season. As a result, the quarterback situation was a mess down the stretch.

After the loss to Georgia, Florida won a difficult game at home against Vanderbilt before winning at South Carolina 48-21.

The Gators were ranked 10th and likely headed to the Citrus Bowl, a letdown after four straight major bowls and two consecutive appearances in the national title game.

FSU was coming to Gainesville, and the Seminoles appeared to be primed for a national championship game. They were ranked second in the Associated Press poll and No. 1 in the USA Today/ESPN coaches' poll.

Florida fans were wondering who would play quarterback. They couldn't have expected what would happen next.

THE GAME OF OUR LIVES
BY NOAH BRINDISE AND DOUG JOHNSON

Brindise: Coach told us Tuesday that he was going to alternate us. We had beaten Vandy and South Carolina but weren't very impressive. I started against South Carolina and we went right down the field and he put Doug in. He struggled for a quarter or so and put me back in. You could tell he was trying to get Doug in the flow.

Johnson: It was a shock to the whole team. I don't know why he did it. Personally, I thought it was the wrong thing to do. There is a reason why nobody else does it. I think it may have affected FSU at first, but after a while they figured it out. They knew, we knew, that if it was a throw I was going to be in there.

Brindise: When he told us we were going to alternate on every play, we looked at each other like, "What is he talking about?" We'd reached the end of our rope with him, yanking us in and out. It was a weird feeling all week. On Friday, Zach Piller, our offensive tackle, looked at me and said, "We're going to beat these guys. I don't know why, but we're going to beat these guys."

Johnson: We had nothing to lose. That made us a dangerous team. And in rivalry games, it doesn't matter which team is better. What I remember going into the game was that there was a lot of doubt in our locker room. They were such a great team. That team never should have lost to us. But as we got closer to the game, the attitude became more like, "They're no different than we are. Let's go beat them."

Brindise: The first play, I threw a pass for eight or nine yards and came running off. My dad knew about it, but an uncle of mine started booing. Then Doug ran a play and I came back in. They were pretty basic on defense. You could tell whether they were playing zone or man. When I was in, they usually played zone. Coach had told us to look at him if we thought they were going to blitz.

Johnson: It was one of those games where we stayed within reach of them throughout. Because we were right there, the confidence on the team grew as the game went on. Fred Taylor had some fumbles but he came right back and made a great run for a touchdown.

Brindise: Fred had a great touchdown run on 18 Bob, which was the play we scored on them a year earlier. It was an inside sweep where he had to make one guy miss and he did.

Johnson: I remember this one deep pass Noah threw to Travis McGriff. It was a play that I was supposed to be in on but Noah was in. Travis told me he thought the ball was never going to come down. It was floating in the air forever.

Brindise: I remember late in the third quarter, we got our play called and we totally whiffed on Andre Wadsworth. He crushed me. Coach was so into the play-calling and he could coach us up between plays. He could tell us everything he wanted. Still, they drove down for what looked like the clinching touchdown, but Mud Harris made a great play knocking Travis Minor out of bounds and they had to settle for a field goal to make it 29-25. We had played so hard we all just said, "Let's go win the game." Their kicker Sebastian Janikowski did the Gator chomp. That pissed everybody off, but what were we going to do?

Johnson: I didn't really see the Gator chomp by Janikowski because Coach had us over in a huddle. He was diagramming a new play on his laminated sheet of paper. He explained what everybody was supposed to do and then said, "Everybody got it?" So we went into the huddle on our own 20 and I asked if everyone knew what they were supposed to do. You could tell two or three guys weren't sure. And I didn't know how to call the play because we didn't have any terminology for what he had drawn up. So I just gave them the formation, the protection call, and the snap count and told them I'd give them a play on the line of scrimmage. When I got to the line, I called "five-semi" which was a flat curl route. But I tugged on my helmet, which was a cue to Jacquez Green to curl and go. I just launched it and he was there. He probably should have scored, but he ran out of gas.

Brindise: For some reason they were playing man coverage and Jacquez got behind them. But we knew we still had to score a touchdown. People were jumping on each other's shoulders. I had my hand on Coach's shoulder running down the sideline. I wanted to know if he wanted me to go in, but he left Doug in. Fred ran it down to the one, then punched it in.

Johnson: Coach was worried about scoring too quickly once we got down to the one, but they only had 10 men on the field so we went ahead and knocked it in.

Brindise: We still had to stop them. We had great kick coverage and everybody on third down was standing on the bench holding hands. Duane Thomas got the interception and we all freaked out. Doug went in for the first play and I told Coach, "I'm taking the last snap."

Johnson: Everyone was going crazy. It was a strange game for me because a quarterback always has pride and wants to be in on every play. It had been a tough year for me so the whole thing was bittersweet. Because we had also just knocked FSU out of a chance to win the national title and beat our rivals and people were going to be talking about that game forever.

Brindise: On the last snap, I ran around a little bit with the ball after taking a knee. Fred grabbed me and pointed to the clock. Four years of getting up in the morning and lifting weights had paid off. It was one of the best days of my life.

THE AFTERMATH

Florida alternated three quarterbacks in the Citrus Bowl, without much success, but the defense led the way to a 21-6 win. Johnson hurt his shoulder in the game and had off-season surgery. For the next two years, he'd battle Palmer for the right to play quarterback.

Johnson led the Gators to an Orange Bowl appearance in 1998 and the SEC Championship Game in '99, but his shoulder fell apart before that game, and he played only a few snaps in a loss to Alabama.

By then Brindise had gone to work as a graduate assistant at Florida and would soon be an NFL assistant when Spurrier went to the Washington Redskins in 2002. Brindise worked for two years there, spent a year at East Carolina and two years as offensive coordinator at UNLV before deciding the coaching profession wasn't for him.

Johnson spent four years in Atlanta, becoming the starter in 2003 when Michael Vick suffered a preseason injury. He has also been a back-up at Tennessee, Cleveland, and Cincinnati.

Brindise wanted to return to his old college town and moved back to Gainesville in 2007 with his wife and two children. He took a job as an orthopedic salesman and may be finished with coaching.

Johnnson and his wife and kids moved to a lake house in Melrose, and Johnson still has some NFL life left in him. He is a backup for the Cincinnati Bengals.

Chapter 7

CHARLIE CASEY

PREGAME

Born in Atlanta, Charlie Casey was surrounded by family. Aunts and uncles were everywhere in the big city, "but in a big city like that you stay on the side you were raised in. Every once in a while you'd venture into the city and go to the movies. Wow."

He was a young boy when his parents were divorced and was raised by his mother and grandmother. Fortunately for Casey, his mom was the athlete in the family.

She was a softball player who was on the company team at Life of Georgia. Every weekend, she'd take Charlie to the park and throw balls around with him—softballs, footballs, baseballs—and the practice would pay off later in hand-eye coordination.

The man who owned Life of Georgia was Rankin Smith, who would later own the Atlanta Falcons.

"He was a big Georgia Bulldog and he wanted me to go to Georgia," Casey said. "I finally asked him one day if I didn't was he going to fire my mom. He said he wouldn't be that way and he actually was really good about it."

Casey played football and baseball in middle school, but once he got to high school he decided the only sports for him were baseball and basketball.

"Baseball was my sport," he said. "I played football in eighth grade and I didn't like it. Our games were on Saturday mornings at eight o'clock and it was cold. So I just decided to play baseball when it was warm and basketball.

"I didn't play football again until I was a junior. All of my buddies were going to spring football practice walking through the gym one day and I was shooting baskets. They all said, 'Come on and play.' So I said, 'OK. I'll go play.'"

Brown High School is no longer there in Atlanta, instead turned into a parking lot. But it would turn out two players from that team who had tremendous success in college—Casey and quarterback Kim King, who starred at Georgia Tech.

The Brown Rebels went 1-8-1 when Casey was a junior.

"That was not very much fun," he said. "We didn't have any seniors that year. But the next year we went 9-1 and it turned out to be fun. The one loss we had kept us from going to the state playoffs.

"I could do one thing—catch the ball. Nobody said back then how fast you were or how tiny my hands were, and they were and still are small. I guess it was just hand-eye coordination from playing baseball for so many years."

Casey flourished in a wide-open offense that was rare for that time. As a split end, he started catching the eyes of college coaches who were looking for a sure-handed receiver.

His first choice was Georgia Tech because he'd always been a fan and always hated Georgia. Duke, Virginia, and other schools were sending letters, but he had always wanted to be an engineer and figured Tech would be the best place for him.

Casey got to meet legendary coach Bobby Dodd on his recruiting visit and also took trips to Clemson, South Carolina, and Georgia among others.

"I went to Florida State 10 times," he said.

But it was a trip to Gainesville that changed his mind. When he boarded the plane in Atlanta early during his senior basketball season, there was a sleeting rain pelting the passengers as they boarded for the flight to Jacksonville.

Charlie Casey and many of his teammates enjoy a Silver Sixties reunion every year in Florida. *University of Florida archives*

"When I landed, it was 72 and beautiful," Casey said. "I was thinking, 'Why would anyone want to leave here?' That sold me."

He was recruited by Florida assistant coach Pepper Rodgers, who was also a Brown high alumnus and lived down the street from Casey.

"He came to our house one time and we were having hot dogs," Casey said with a laugh. "He ate about four hot dogs faster than I ever saw anybody eat, talking all the time. He sold me on it and the weather sold me on it, and Florida had a good engineering school as well, although I never went into engineering because it was too damn hard."

Casey played on the freshman team at UF and played defensive end in scrimmages against the varsity. It was then that he got a taste of college football and wondered if he had made a mistake in his choice of colleges.

There was a scrimmage when quarterback Larry Libertore came wide on an option and Casey thought he was going to smash the diminutive player. Instead, Casey was left grasping at air.

But what was really frustrating was the Florida offense.

"It was two tight ends for three yards and a cloud of dust," he said. "And I was playing defensive end, and at 165 then I wasn't going to stop anybody."

But he stuck it out, playing both ways as a sophomore, the last year that college players had to go both ways.

"Coach Gene Ellenson was the defensive coach and he was a genius," he said. "It was like, 'How can I hide Casey because he's gotta play?'

"We played Auburn and all they did was sweep right and sweep left with Tucker Fredrickson, who was a moose at 220 pounds. Coach Ellenson told me that when they come at you, stay on his outside shoulder as long as you can. I'd stayed outside, and he'd take me to the bench."

Casey had worked his way up from fifth team to second team as a sophomore, but didn't know how his career was about to change. Rodgers had been pushing head coach Ray Graves to open up the offense and Graves had found the guy to do that, signing Steve Spurrier to play quarterback.

"He sure did, thank God," Casey said.

In his junior season at UF, Florida split time at quarterback between Tommy Shannon and Spurrier and installed Casey as the "lonesome end," meaning he didn't have to come to the huddle and instead would get the plays from hand signals. It was something the Gator coaches had seen in 1962 in a 28-21 loss to Duke in Jacksonville.

Casey flourished in the new offense as a junior with Spurrier doing most of the passing. His senior year would provide an even better season.

With Spurrier as a junior and Casey a senior, Florida was going through an up-and-down season. A loss to Mississippi State in the second game and the usual loss at Auburn when the Gators were ranked seventh knocked Florida out of any chance to win the SEC.

A 16-13 loss to Miami didn't keep Florida from accepting a bowl bid to the Sugar Bowl, UF's first major bowl game.

But before that game could be played, there was one final regular-season game against the hated Seminoles in Gainesville.

THE GAME OF MY LIFE
BY CHARLIE CASEY

When I look back on my career at Florida, the game that sticks out the most in my mind is my senior year against Florida State. Georgia and FSU were the two teams I hated the most. I'd always hated Georgia and FSU, you get it bred into you when you are at Florida. Those are the bad guys.

The FSU game that year was special because they had beaten us in my junior year for the first time when we wore "Go For Seven"—on our jerseys because they hadn't beaten us the first six times we played. That was bad news. Can you imagine someone doing that now? It was like waving a red flag. You just kill yourself.

The thing I remember about this game was getting the crud knocked out of me about half the time. Both sides just beat each other to a pulp—clean, but really hard-hitting. If you ran a pass pattern and the ball was overthrown, you had better prepare to get hit, and you really got hit and the refs would say, "OK, just keep it clean."

I caught five or six passes during the game, but late in the game they went down and scored, and we were behind 17-16. We went on offense with only a few minutes remaining, but it wasn't a desperation-type thing. It was calm, actually, even when they went ahead. Steve called the plays and we just methodically went down the field.

Bill Campbell was their cornerback. He was a sub 9.7 sprinter and I was running 11 flat. But Steve called a down-and-out pattern—94 block pass—a sprint out behind the tackle.

I ran down and started the out move, and out of the corner of my eye I saw the corner starting to move. As I came out of the break, I looked back at Steve and he was rolling out. He waved me down the field so I went, "OK. Zoom."

As I turned up, the corner went right by me. He was going to jump the route. Steve saw it coming so he waved me down the field. There was nobody there and I just ran down the field.

He threw the ball and it went right through the sun. Oh God, where is it? The year before I dropped a pass at Doak Campbell that Steve threw.

It went right through my hands. I didn't even touch it. I guess I just misjudged the flight of the ball because as I looked back it went right through my hands. And when it hit the ground, it was spinning perfectly because I didn't even touch it.

So I was thinking, "Oh God, here I go again. Where is the ball? Don't be the goat. You gotta catch this thing."

About three or four yards before it got to me, it came out of the sun. I could see it! Hallelujah! I saw it leave his hand thinking, "Oh man, this is great," and it disappeared.

I caught that thing and thought, "I want to cherish you, ball." It was great.

And then Allen Trammell picked off a pass and ran it back for another score, and we won 30-17. Trammell takes all the credit.

I didn't know that Steve had seen the flag and they had jumped offsides and he knew he had a free play.

My mother and grandmother came to every game. We had dinner with them and 12 or 15 Phi Delts. We went back to their house and had a good time.

I've got a picture from that game of a pass, a slant pass, that broke the SEC receiving and school records. It was just a great day.

THE AFTERMATH

Casey was drafted out of high school by Milwaukee but turned it down because his mother insisted that he go to college and get a degree. He was drafted again by the Kansas City Royals after playing baseball as a junior at UF.

But it was after his senior season that he experienced the wild world of a football draft with two leagues competing.

It was during Sugar Bowl week that he was contacted by the Oilers and told he could sign with the team, walk across the street to a bank and fill a suitcase with money.

"I told him, 'I can't do that. I can't let the team down.' If I'd gotten caught, I'd be letting them down. They had paid for my mom, grandma, and uncle to come to New Orleans. It was a big temptation because I didn't have two nickels."

Casey was approached after the Sugar Bowl loss to Missouri by Atlanta. He told the Falcons to talk to his agent, Willie O'Neal.

"We were in the hotel and they made a good offer," Casey said. "I took it, which may have been a mistake. I left the room, and later Willie told me Houston had called back with an offer for 20 grand more."

Casey never played in the NFL, suffering two torn ligaments in his ankle when he stepped in a hole during a minor league football game in Huntsville, Alabama. Once he was cut and also failed the physicals for the armed services because of the ankle, he moved to Melbourne and began coaching in Titusville.

Two years later, he was offered a job at a new school in Fort Myers called Riverdale. At the age of 27, he was named head coach and athletic director at Riverdale High.

After five years, he opened a golf and tennis shop, then went into the stock broker business.

Casey's career continues to flourish in Fort Myers where he has been a stock broker for 25 years. He still attends many Gator football games and still enjoys beating FSU.

Chapter 8

CRIS COLLINSWORTH

FLORIDA VS. MARYLAND
DECEMBER 20, 1980
TANGERINE BOWL
ORLANDO, FLORIDA

PREGAME

Cris Collinsworth was born in Dayton, Ohio, but moved to Eau Gallie, Florida, and then Melbourne, Florida, as a young boy. Just before his seventh grade year, the Collinsworth family moved to nearby Titusville, Florida, where Collinsworth would excel in football, basketball, and baseball.

As a Pop Warner player, he was 119 pounds in a 120-pound league so he was lined up at offensive and defensive tackle.

"But I kept running wind sprints," he said. "I knew if I didn't let anybody tackle me, I wouldn't have to go back to the line."

He won the quarterback job in junior high and stayed at that position all the way through high school. His speed was his best asset, as Collinsworth won the state 100-yard dash title as a junior.

It was during his high school years that he began to study film as a teacher's assistant to head coach Jay Donnelly.

"It was great for me," he said. "I was spending all the time with the head coach. We'd put together the game plans. I [soon] understood the game of football more than [most other players]."

It was during his junior season in a state playoff game that he learned a lesson in football.

Back then, high school football had a penetration rule in overtime. In a game against Tampa Jesuit, the team that ended up on the opponent's side of the 50 would win at the end of overtime.

"The rules were so crazy," he said. "We had practiced batting down balls, because if you intercepted one and got tackled, you lost yardage. They threw a pass, and I had it in my hands. But I batted it down. There wasn't a soul in sight. I could have walked backwards into the end zone.

"That was the last time I followed the rules."

As a senior, the speedy quarterback was at the top of everyone's wish list. But he knew where he was going.

He had long been a fan of the Florida Gators, but that didn't keep Collinsworth from taking his official visits.

"Bear Bryant was in my house, Bobby Bowden went to every game," he said. "When I went to Kentucky, I met Adolph Rupp. At Southern Cal, O.J. Simpson took me around. I was going to Florida no matter what. I was just seeing the world."

His arrival in Gainesville couldn't have come at a better time for Florida coach Doug Dickey, who had produced some powerhouse teams that failed to live up to expectations.

Dickey's situation was dicey to say the least and he would last only two more seasons. But with Collinsworth on campus, the savior had arrived.

It was during his freshman year that Collinsworth was handed his nickname—Cadillac. It wasn't his style or his car or his lofty status as a high school wonderboy that earned him the nickname.

He wishes that would have been the case.

"There's a better story I could tell about that, but it wouldn't be the truth," Collinsworth said. "My first day there we were standing in line getting our equipment. I couldn't find a helmet that fit, and I was trying on a bunch of them. Finally, one of the big defensive linemen who was waiting yelled at me, 'Come on, find something that will fit that big Cadillac head of yours.' The name just stuck after that."

Cris Collinsworth is better known these days for his work in television than his career in football. *The Gainesville Sun*

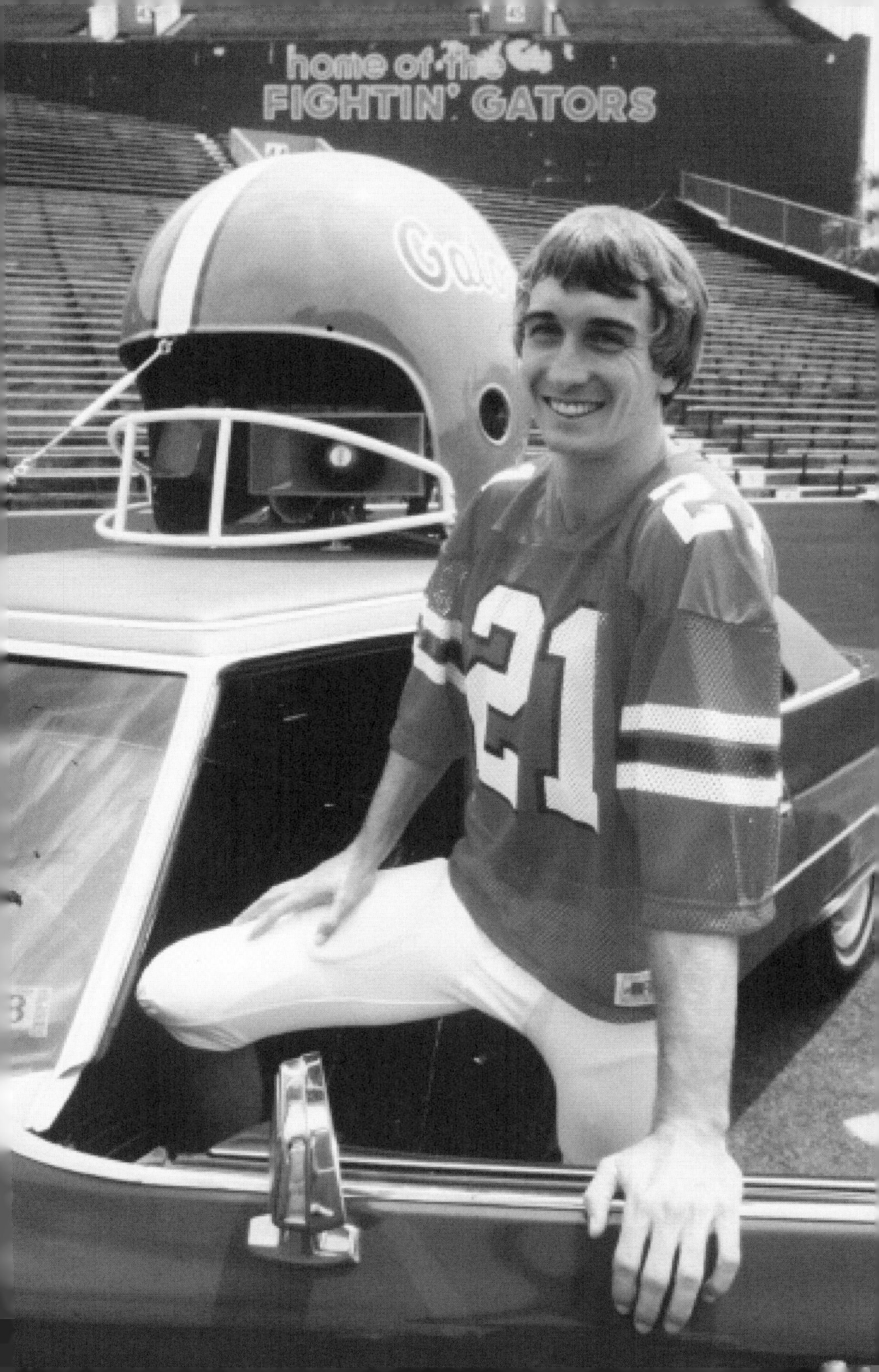
home of the
FIGHTIN' GATORS

Florida at the time was still in the last days of the wishbone attack and Collinsworth saw some time as a back-up at quarterback. In one game, he set a record that will never be broken.

Against Rice in the first game of his college career. Collinsworth rolled right from his own 1-yard line and found Derrick Gaffney open behind the defense. The result was an NCAA record-tying 99-yard touchdown pass.

Other than that, it was a pretty uneventful freshman season for Collinsworth. But there was one play that inadvertently changed the direction of his career.

"It was a key moment against Georgia and they put me in," he said. "I scrambled around and tried to jump over the only defender who was in my way. He caught me with the very tip of his finger on my toe and I went straight down.

"I still wonder to this day if I had run for 50 yards on that play if I would have stayed at quarterback. I wouldn't have been in the NFL and I wouldn't have become a broadcaster."

When Collinsworth broke his hand near the end of his freshman year, the Florida coaches tried him at cornerback.

"I knew I could cover those guys," he said. "We were playing FSU and they ran a draw with Larry Key. He put a move on me and I didn't even come close to him. That was my last play at defensive back."

The Florida coaches tried Collinsworth at running back during practice before his sophomore season because of his speed, but again fate stepped in.

"I was on a blitz pick-up and David Galloway, who was a tremendous defensive tackle, picked me up and threw me into the quarterback," Collinsworth said. "He almost killed me. Steve Spurrier was an assistant then, and he wanted me to try wingback."

Collinsworth led the team in receiving, but by his junior season, Dickey and Spurrier were both gone. Charley Pell was the new coach. Collinsworth again led the team in receiving, but the Gators went 0-10-1.

"It was such a huge transition," he said. "We went to a drop-back passing team and we didn't have any quarterbacks. A ton of things conspired against that team. But I've always said that year was good for me. I came in thinking that by myself we could win at least one game. And it taught me how to deal with the media no matter what was happening.

"I would stand there after every loss and answer all the questions. It was a tough year because even the professors were making jokes. Here I am in an economics class and the guy thinks he's a stand-up comedian. But you go to college to learn in a lot of ways. I learned how to handle adversity."

Florida was supposed to be better in Pell's second year. The Gators wasted no time getting that first win for their coach with a 41-13 trouncing of California in the opener. After a 3-0 start, an injury to quarterback Bob Hewko put a damper on things, but freshman Wayne Peace replaced Hewko and guided the Gators to three straight wins.

Even after losses to Miami and FSU to close the season, Florida would go bowling for the first time since 1976 against Maryland in the Tangerine Bowl.

It was a chance for the seniors to go out on a high note.

THE GAME OF MY LIFE
BY CRIS COLLINSWORTH

The thing about 1980 was that it was my whole draft year. The thing I remember most was that the Hula Bowl invited me to play before the season. That was a big deal for me.

But I only had about 10 catches in the first five games. I remember they posted the SEC stats on the board and my name was nowhere to be found.

So I got a notice from the Hula Bowl that I was no longer invited. That really fired me up. I had 30 catches in the last five games and led the SEC in receiving. Then, the Hula Bowl wanted me. I gave them the old Florida finger and said forget it. The Japan Bowl wanted me, and I'd never been to Japan so I accepted.

But first we had this bowl game to play, which was new to us. We got down to Orlando and Arnold Palmer invited a bunch of us to his condo at Bay Hill. We were all kind of intimidated. The first thing he said was, "You guys know you are going to get crushed in this game, don't you?"

I mean, we hadn't even said hello and I was already in an argument with him. He was just giving us the needle but I didn't realize it. I was ready to go.

The game set up beautifully for us. Maryland played that old wide-tackle six and they only had three defensive backs on the field. If we didn't throw it all over those guys, we were never going to throw it.

The big thing for us seniors is that we wanted to put an exclamation point on the turnaround. For my recruiting class, to go through 0-10-1 and do what we did the next year, well, Florida has never looked back since.

We hit them with a couple of hitches early in the game and you could tell the defensive back covering me was getting frustrated. He started cheating on me. So I told Wayne Peace, our quarterback, I was going to fake the hitch and go long.

Well, he took it hook, line, and sinker. I've never been so wide open in my life. That touchdown gave us an early lead and we kept throwing it on them. Wayne had a great game. He was always so poised the way he handled the team.

He threw me another touchdown pass in the third quarter, and we went on to win 35-20. It was a great way to go out, and it was a great game for me to go out, eight catches for 166 yards.

Now Boomer Esiason, who was on the Maryland team, is always giving me a hard time about a victory lap I took after the game. I always tell him he's out of his mind, that never happened. He said I was running around the stadium and the fans were doing the wave with me.

But that's not what happened.

In retrospect, I know what happened. There were only a couple of minutes left in the game and we had it in hand. They announced that I was the MVP of the game and they wanted me to do an interview.

It was set up on the other sideline, so I did run around to that sideline to do the interview. Johnny Unitas was doing the game and I wanted a chance to be interviewed by him. It was really cool.

So that's the way we finished, with a bowl victory and an 8-4 record after going 0-10-1 the year before. And I was the MVP.

But the worst thing that happened to me was not going to the Hula Bowl. The scouts didn't go to Japan. I think that had a lot to do with why I wasn't drafted until the second round.

THE AFTERMATH

Collinsworth was drafted in the second round by Cincinnati and had a stellar career with the Bengals.

He was selected to the Pro Bowl three times and played in two Super Bowls. For his career. Collinsworth caught 417 passes for 6,698 yards and 36 touchdowns.

In seven playoff games including two Super Bowl losses, Collinsworth caught 21 passes for 354 yards.

He signed with the USFL Tampa Bay Bandits in 1985 but failed his physical because of a bad ankle and returned to the Bengals to finish out his career.

It was after his playing career that a new one presented itself. Collinsworth began doing a radio show on WLW in Cincinnati with Bob Trumpy. His ease and clever wit behind the microphone led to an opportunity in television on *Inside the NFL* on HBO.

Collinsworth joined NBC in 1990 as a color analyst and became one of the pregame hosts in 1996. In 1998, he moved to Fox and covered a Super Bowl for the network before returning to NBC in 2006.

He continues to work on the HBO show as well as with NBC.

Collinsworth lives in Fort Thomas, Kentucky, near Cincinnati with his wife and four children. His busy schedule has forced him to withdraw from a pair of charity golf tournaments that bore his name in Florida, but he is still involved in many charities both in the Cincinnati area and around the country.

Chapter 9

BRAD CULPEPPER

FLORIDA VS. LSU
OCTOBER 7, 1989
TIGER STADIUM
BATON ROUGE, LOUISIANA

PREGAME

John Broward Culpepper II was his birth name, but he was always known as Brad. Born in Orlando, Florida, Culpepper was named for his grandfather, the first chancellor of the Florida Board of Regents that supervised the state's colleges and universities. His father Bruce was the captain of the 1962 Gator team that upset Penn State in the Gator Bowl. His brother, uncle, mother, and sister also attended Florida.

Culpepper grew up in Tallahassee and the pedigree of athletics took. At Leon High, he was a multisport star, lettering in football, baseball, weightlifting and track.

"I was probably a better baseball player than a football player," he said.

As a pitcher in high school, he won 46 games and was first-team all-state and was inducted into the state's baseball Hall of Fame.

As a football player, he started from his first game as a freshman through his senior season.

"Gene Cox was my coach and he was a tough son of a gun," Culpepper said. "But he instilled a toughness in me and a work ethic that separated me from the rest in the future."

Culpepper was third-team all-state as a sophomore, first team as a junior and an All-American as a senior. He played offensive guard, defensive end, defensive tackle, tight end, offensive tackle, fullback, and nose guard during his high school career.

When it came time to pick a college, he took visits to Alabama, Auburn, Florida State, Florida, and Notre Dame.

"I crossed out Alabama and Auburn, because who wants to live in Alabama?" he said. "I didn't want to be a farmer. I eliminated FSU because I wanted to get away from home. So it was down to Florida and Notre Dame. Lou Holtz was recruiting me and he promised they'd win a national championship. I'll be damned if they didn't do it the next year.

"When I visited, the girls at Florida blew away the girls at Notre Dame. My brother was at Florida and the pulse of the state was leaning that way. That class of 1987 was a great class with Emmitt Smith. By the time we got to 1989, 11 of the 22 starters were from that class. All of those guys were talking through the recruiting process and we just decided, 'Let's all go to Florida.'"

But before he would start playing at Florida, Culpepper had to fight for his life.

At the end of his senior year at Leon, Culpepper contracted a virus that infected his spine. Doctors in Tallahassee shipped him to Shands Hospital in Gainesville to try to figure out what the problem was.

"I was real sick. They thought I was going to die," he said. "Football wasn't even a possibility. I graduated one day and was at Shands the next day. I had spiking fevers of 104 degrees. I lost a lot of weight, down to 215 pounds from 255. But they put me on a medicine that worked, and after spending four or five weeks in the hospital I was good to go."

At 215, however, he wasn't going to play as a true freshman. Florida coaches had planned to play Culpepper at center or guard, but he spent the first year as a redshirt.

"They threw me in on defense, and I was super quick at 215," he said.

As a redshirt freshman, Culpepper played behind Jeff Roth at nose tackle and started in Florida's win over Illinois in the All-American Bowl. The following year, Culpepper was the starter.

Brad Culpepper was an undersized tackle in college and the NFL but used quickness, brains, and heart to be successful. *The Gainesville Sun*

Florida was recovering from the probation years that crippled the program because of violations committed by Charley Pell's staff. The 1987 class was the first full class in three years.

"We went into the 1989 season with high expectations even though we were really young," Culpepper said. "We thought we were good to go."

The season started with a whimper. Florida lost at home 24-19 to Ole Miss as embattled quarterback Kyle Morris threw three interceptions. But the Gators got back on track with three straight wins heading to Baton Rouge.

While Florida's players were feeling good about themselves in the first week of October, they had no idea what was going on behind the scenes.

As part of its investigation of the Florida basketball program, the NCAA had uncovered several minor violations in the football program, the most egregious being an alleged payment of defensive back Jarvis Williams' child support that was due.

Coach Galen Hall to this day says that the envelope he sent to Palatka, Florida—Williams' home town—contained only paperwork.

But UF officials had the excuse they needed to dump their coach.

They met with Hall during the week and told him the LSU game would be his last. When *Gainesville Sun* reporters learned of the rumors that Hall was out, two of them went to the coach's home two days before the trip to Louisiana to ask him about the possibility that he was no longer the Gator coach.

Hall said he couldn't talk about it, but he would address it on the Sunday after the game.

The players—and just about everyone else in the Gator Nation— were oblivious to what was going on behind closed doors. They just wanted to win a football game.

THE GAME OF MY LIFE
BY BRAD CULPEPPER

We had started out with that loss at home when Kyle threw three picks, but we were good. Kyle was playing much better and our defense was ranked No. 1 in the nation.

Of course, we had no idea what was going on with Galen. I've asked players since that night and nobody had any inkling that this was his last game. We just wanted to keep the momentum going because we were starting to really play well.

The biggest thing I remember was that it was really loud. I always liked playing in Baton Rouge because their fans were so passionate about their team. They were struggling and their backs were against the wall so we knew they would come out ready to play.

The crowd was pretty intense. It was a night game but that didn't matter to me. I was never one to sweat it either way. If it was an early game, you get up and go play. If it was at night, you just played later. One way or another, you had a game to play.

But night games there, they really get all fired up and they were when the Gators came to town.

I remember being jacked up with the crowd and all because they were jacked up, too. We were so good on defense, and early in the game Richard Fain got an interception. Their quarterback was Tommy Hodson and he was really good, but I got to him five or six times in the game.

Huey Richardson was flying around at end and linebacker Jerry Odom was everywhere. We shut them down.

We gave the offense opportunities to score, but they were having a difficult time getting the ball in the end zone. It should have been at least 14-0 at the half, but it was only 3-0. We were disappointed not being up by a lot more, but we felt like defensively we were holding our own.

We blocked a couple of punts, Timmy Paulk got one, and we got a bunch of turnovers. But Emmitt fumbled one time. Neither team really had a sustained drive. They hit a swing pass to Eddie Fuller and he broke a tackle and scored. Emmitt popped a 25-yard run for our touchdown.

We stopped them in the third quarter on fourth-and-a-foot at our 10. And in the fourth quarter, we did it again. They were running out of time on the play clock and should have called a time-out, but Hodson rushed to the line and got the snap really quick. We shoved them into the backfield and we made a big defensive stand.

It was 13-13 and there was 1:20 to play. Kyle was really drilling it. He moved us down the field and they called for a run with Emmitt, maybe trying to surprise them. But rather than go down and get the field goal team on the field, he stretched it out wide. He ran to the right and ran to the right and ran to the right. He didn't get out of bounds.

The clock was ticking down, eight seconds, seven seconds. Kyle got everybody up to the line and threw it out of bounds. The clock said zeroes and they started celebrating like they had won the game when it was really tied. I found that strange.

Galen started arguing that there should be time on the clock, that there was a second left. The officials got together and they agreed. Mike Archer, who was their coach, was throwing a hissy fit on the sidelines.

John David Francis was our kicker. He had missed one earlier in the game. So they had put Arden Czyzewski in for an extra point and he had just barely made it. But he went out to try this 41-yard field goal to win the game. We were all wondering why John David wasn't out there.

He kicked it from the right hash and it started moving left and moving left. He made it by the skin of his teeth. And we started celebrating like crazy.

After the game, Galen got a bit emotional. He was telling the team how nobody thought we could do it, nobody expected us to do it and how we had our backs against the wall. We didn't know what to think because he was so emotional. We just thought it was a big win.

On Sunday at the team meeting, it all went down. then, two days later, they suspended Kyle and some other players for gambling. It was all just an internal witch-hunt, but we knew our season was over. It was a shame because we had a really good team.

THE AFTERMATH

With Morris suspended and Hall fired, the season took a downturn. The win over LSU put the Gators into the top 25 and they won the next two games against Vanderbilt and New Mexico under interim coach Gary Darnell, who was the defensive coordinator. But a devastating last-second loss at Auburn was followed by a 17-10 loss to Georgia and a 24-17 loss to Florida State.

The Gators played in the Freedom Bowl in Anaheim and were hammered by Washington 34-7. Speculation swirled that Steve Spurrier was about to become the new coach at UF and on New Year's Eve, 1989, it became official.

"Steve Spurrier inherited a stacked team," Culpepper said. "That class of '87, we were all juniors and seniors and we were really good on defense."

Indeed, Florida had the best record in the conference in 1990, but UF was ineligible to win the SEC or play in a bowl game because of NCAA sanctions. The following year, Florida was the best team in the SEC and had no sanctions to worry about.

The Gators ended up winning against FSU 14-9 to close out the '91 season as Culpepper, who was named to several All-America teams, played a dominating game while harassing Seminole quarterback Casey Weldon. A loss in the Sugar Bowl couldn't dampen the best season to that point in UF history.

Culpepper was drafted in the 10th round by Minnesota, was cut in 1994, and went to Tampa Bay, where he enjoyed six seasons as a starting defensive tackle, anchoring one of the best defenses in pro football. After being released by the Bucs, he spent a year with Chciago before retiring from football.

He finished his law degree and is now a practicing attorney in Tampa where he lives with his wife, Monica, a former UF homecoming queen, and their three children.

Chapter 10

JUDD DAVIS

FLORIDA VS. GEORGIA
OCTOBER 30, 1993
GATOR BOWL
JACKSONVILLE, FLORIDA

PREGAME

Judd Davis was born in Orange, California, but his family moved to Edwardsburg, Michigan, just across the border between Michigan and Indiana, shortly after he was born. As a result, he grew up a big fan of the Fighting Irish of Notre Dame.

"We'd go down to games there and I played on a soccer team that was called the Junior Irish," he said. "Soccer was huge up there. Where I grew up, you didn't play Little League baseball or youth football. You played soccer. If you did it the other way around, you were considered kind of a dork. Where I went to school, the soccer players were considered kind of the studs, not the football players."

He had a knack for kicking the soccer ball farther than anyone else on his team, but had no real interest in football until his father took him to a field across from the family's house one day when Davis was in the seventh grade. Ben Davis brought a football with him, held it upright and told his son to kick it.

"He paced it off and he knew right then I could be a kicker," Davis said.

Davis played football in middle school, kicking field goals and playing some wide receiver. Before his freshman year of high school, he attended Auburn's kicking camp even though he wasn't old enough to be there.

"We fudged on it," he said.

But before he could kick in high school, the family moved to Florida. His parents had grown up in Ocala, and when his father was offered a choice of where to live he chose his hometown. It was there that his grandfather "Smack 'Em" Davis was an every-down player for Ocala Forest High and eventually walked on at Florida.

After spending so much time in Michigan, Ocala was a culture shock for the Davis brothers.

"My brother and I didn't know anybody," he said. "I remember going to football practice and I couldn't understand what some of the players were saying. I remember distinctly thinking. 'This is bizarre.' I'd never heard anyone talking like that."

At 120 pounds, kicking was the way to go to get a college scholarship, but an injury in his junior year basically ended that dream. By the time he got to his senior season, most colleges had already lined up any kickers they wanted to sign.

Davis went 7-of-8 on field goals, but missing his junior season "killed me."

His friends suggested Davis try to go to a smaller school where he'd get a chance to play. He wanted to try Florida. When his friends insisted that was a pipe dream, that a skinny kid from Ocala couldn't just walk on at Florida, it made Davis want it even more.

So he sent a tape to Florida where a handful of place-kickers were going to be given the chance.

Florida had a new coach in Steve Spurrier, who had a different approach to things. There were no favorites for any jobs. Everyone was new to him like he was new to them.

"Just a bunch of guys with names taped on their helmets," Davis said. "They didn't know the starting linebacker any more than they knew me."

Davis had spent a year at Central Florida Community College to get his academics in order before heading to Gainesville. This was the opportunity he had been waiting for, but it would take a detour.

Florida had a solid kicker in Arden Czyzewski, so Davis went out for the punting job. He knew Florida was looking for a punter and he performed well enough to be the top punter. But when the season started, it was Czyzewski who was assigned the double duty of being the place-kicker and the punter.

Davis almost hit the field during his freshman year. During Florida's 61-14 homecoming win over Southwestern Louisiana, he was told to get ready for the next extra point.

He was confused. Thinking he was going to redshirt and not sure of the rules, he turned to Czyzewski, who told him not to do it because he'd lose his redshirt. He didn't and didn't, giving him four remaining years of eligibility.

"And then they signed Shayne Edge," Davis said.

Edge was a star punter at Lake City Columbia High north of Gainesville who would soon become best friends with Davis. But in 1991, they fought for the same job as the Gator punter.

"Shayne was supposed to be the big savior because they hadn't seen a spiraled punt in years since Ray Criswell was kicking in the mid-1980s," Davis said. "Coach Spurrier told Shayne he had the first two punts in our opener against San Jose State.

"Well, he goes out for the first one and shanks it. I mean, a complete shank. You should have heard the boos. He was white as a ghost when he came off the field. I told him to relax, but at the same time I was thinking, 'Sweet, I'm going in.' The next punt, it's a high snap and Shayne makes this athletic play to go up and get it and then kicks a 61-yard punt. They gave him a standing ovation. I remember sitting down knowing I wasn't getting in. The next week at practice, I was back kicking field goals."

With Czyzewski graduating, the place-kicking job was up for grabs in 1992. But Florida had signed a decorated kicker in Bart Edmiston, who was great in practice but shaky once he went across the street into The Swamp.

By now, Davis was wondering if a transfer wasn't the best thing for him.

"I wanted to go talk to Coach Spurrier, but everyone was telling me that you don't do that," Davis said. "I finally told Edge, 'I'm going.' I went in there and told him I felt I was kicking better than Bart. I remember him looking at me wondering why this kicker was in his office. He told me to just keep kicking."

Florida was at South Carolina the following Saturday. In the first half, Edmiston missed a 30-yard field goal attempt. Sitting in the hallway at halftime eating a banana, Davis was startled when Spurrier approached the kickers. With typical Spurrier candor, he said simply, "Bart, you're out. Judd, you're up."

Davis went out before the rest of the team and started warming up. The frustration of not being able to kick turned to adrenaline and he started nailing everything. The Gator fans in attendance started cheering while at the same time wondering who this guy was making 50-yarders.

Davis made three extra points in the game and was named the starter. He made a 47-yard field goal the next week against Vanderbilt and was handed a game ball by Spurrier.

He would enter the 1993 season as Florida's starter and was off to a strong start when the 5-1 Gators went to Jacksonville for the annual game against Georgia.

Florida had won a thriller in Lexington, beaten Tennessee at home and demolished LSU in Baton Rouge. Ranked fourth in the nation, the Gators lost a controversial heartbreaker in Auburn 38-35 to spoil their perfect season.

After a bye week, UF was set to take on a Georgia team that had a strong-armed quarterback in Eric Zeier. But the tide had changed in the series with Spurrier holding a 3-0 record against the Bulldogs as the Gator coach. Winning No. 4 would keep the hopes for another SEC title alive.

THE GAME OF MY LIFE
BY JUDD DAVIS

This was my favorite game because people who voted for me in the balloting for the Lou Groza Award said that game right there won you the Lou Groza Award. I really appreciated winning that award at the end of the season because I had gone from nothing to being named the best kicker in the nation.

Judd Davis is arguably the best golfer of any Gator football player who has graduated from UF. *The Gainesville Sun*

That game is always so different up in Jacksonville. Bottles are flying in, hitting the side of the bus. People are dragging stuffed Gators behind them.

I hadn't missed a field goal that year, but I remember seeing in the weather report that it was going to rain. As a kicker, I hated playing in the Gator Bowl because they let the grass grow so tall. It was the thickest field of anywhere. You go to Florida Field and you could hit a 1-iron off of it. In that stadium, you'd put the ball down to kick it, and you couldn't see the bottom stripe. If you didn't go down and get it you'd kick that little squib to the left.

I remember coming into the game, in the pregame it rained 30 minutes before the game. Shayne and I and our long-snapper Harold Monk walked out and you couldn't see 20 yards across the field it was raining so hard.

We ran out and all the drunken people had their shirts off and there was a river flowing down the steps. I don't know if I've ever seen it rain that hard. We were looking at each other with water up to our ankles wondering if we should even kick. I told Edge, "We're not going to kick any field goals today, you're going to be punting all day." He punted once in the game and I remember they didn't catch it and it plugged. We were just out there laughing.

We finally went in during pregame and half the team just stopped and looked at us. We were soaked. They didn't realize how hard it was raining. They changed to long spikes. Shayne and I just were trying to figure out how to keep our feet dry. We started out using baggies. Our shoes were going to get wet, but we wanted to keep our socks dry so we put on a baggie up to our ankles and taped it. Brilliant plan we had. It didn't work.

Going from the sideline to the benches there was a drain and it got clogged so you'd wade through this lake to the bench. It was comical.

So the game got going and we got stopped in their territory and someone yelled, "Field goal, field goal." We went out there and it was just muddy. Shayne would push the mud around to give us a tee. Whenever I kicked I had to go down and get it and it would send a little wave of mud up into Shayne's face. I'd kick and look up at Edge and his face would be just black. I'd say, "I'm sorry, dude." He just said, "You keep putting them through and you can keep spraying me."

I made three in the first half. None of them were long—29, 27, and 36 yards—and then a 31-yarder in the second half. To go 4-for-4, Shayne did a great job, and Monk, he was best center I ever saw.

The last one was a big one, gave us a 33-20 lead. Coach Spurrier would never hit me on the helmet. He was always of the mind-set that that's your job. But I remember after the last one he met me out on the field and said that was big, that was big. I remember thinking that was big if he was saying that.

On TV the next morning he said that was the biggest kick of the game. He also said the reason I was able to make those kicks is because I was a golfer and I knew how to get a wedge and dig it out of bad lies. "Judd got his foot wedge in there," he said.

I did used to golf a lot when I was kicking bad. I was laying in bed two days before the first game, and I was in a slump. I was coming too far inside. I just decided I was going to try to kick a fade. I tried three kicks and they all went dead straight.

It was a great game, and it's the one where Anthone Lott, our defensive back, called timeout right before they threw a touchdown pass. It was clear as a bell that he did it. Eric Zeier put on a display that day. Danny Wuerffel struggled to hold onto the ball and Coach told him that Zeier wasn't having a problem with it. He put Terry Dean in at quarterback and he did a great job.

Last play of the game, Zeier threw behind the guy and it was over. I jumped onto the pile and Zeier was kneeling on the ground. I remember thinking he played a hell of a game and didn't deserve that.

I went to the Jacksonville Landing that night and I didn't realize how big a deal it was that I had made those four field goals. People were picking me up and putting me on their shoulders. After the game, I looked at the stats and I didn't even realize I had made four field goals. And seeing my parents outside the stadium after the game, it was a great feeling.

It was a strange feeling to wait on every snap and hesitate because I wanted to make sure Edge got it down. I was just praying they weren't coming but they couldn't get any traction to really rush me. Mud was flying off the ball on every kick. It really was a special game.

THE AFTERMATH

Davis helped Florida win the SEC in '93 and go on to the Sugar Bowl where the Gators dismantled West Virginia 41-7.

In his senior season, Davis had another strong year that included kicking the game-winning extra point in the SEC Championship Game against Alabama.

During his four seasons at Florida, the Gators won three SEC titles, the first three official ones in school history.

After a couple of shots with Seattle and Miami in training camp, Davis returned to Ocala where he still lives today. He is an exceptional golfer and has talked to Florida's current kickers about the art of the profession.

Chapter 11

CHRIS DOERING

FLORIDA VS. KENTUCKY
SEPTEMBER 11, 1993
COMMONWEALTH STADIUM
LEXINGTON, KENTUCKY

PREGAME

There has never been a bigger Gator fan than Chris Doering. As a child growing up in Gainesville, he was a fixture at all kinds of UF sporting events.

"I went to all the Gator stuff," he said. "Gymnastics, baseball, all of the football games. That was the cool thing about growing up in Gainesville—you had the opportunity to go to so many different sporting events."

But as a child, Doering's parents didn't want him to play football because they worried that the skinny boy would get hurt. He played soccer instead, running through the fields at what is now Butler Plaza.

His parents finally relented when Doering was in seventh grade at P.K. Yonge, where he had been going to school since the fourth grade. He was the junior varsity placekicker, and in the last game was inserted at wide receiver, a move that was the first of many that changed his life.

The following year, he started for the junior varsity, then was moved up to varsity as a freshman. He was also a skilled basketball player who played varsity in his junior and senior years. In his senior year, P.K. Yonge won the state championship.

"That's one of the things where I learned the most about competitiveness," he said. "Randall Leath was my coach and he wasn't the most friendly guy in the world although we're great friends now. But he taught me how to push myself and to manipulate my mind. He taught me to expect more out of myself than I thought I had."

When Doering was a sophomore, P.K. Yonge dropped out of district play to face a more reasonable schedule. The UF charter school was tired of losing to bigger and better teams like Union County and Williston.

Doering flourished in his senior season. The Blue Wave lost only one game to Florida High that year. But it was a devastating loss to Doering.

"I was crying on the field after the game," he said. "We had been notorious for losing but we changed the perception. I wish we had played in the districts that year because we had a lot of good players."

At 6-foot-4, 155 pounds, Doering was hardly coveted by major college programs. He had some interest from non-scholarship schools and considered going to Kentucky Wesleyan.

Florida showed little interest. Steve Spurrier sent assistant Jim Collins to P.K. Yonge's bowl game against Union County, but Doering believes it was a token gesture. In the first half, he dropped a pair of slant passes. Collins left at halftime and missed a big second half by the wide receiver.

"I was heartbroken," Doering said. "It was the first time someone told me I wasn't good enough. It had always been my dream as a kid to be Cris Collinsworth. I always knew it would be the case."

Doering never missed a Gator Fan Day and had his picture taken with many UF players over the years—including Collinsworth. But the school of his dreams wasn't offering.

There was some interest from Florida State to come out as a walk-on, but while attending a Florida-FSU baseball game Doering felt sick to his stomach listening to the Seminole War Chant. He decided then he would be a Gator, one way or another.

"I got a break because Coach Spurrier gave me preferred walk-on status which meant I didn't have to try out," he said. "I thought about FSU because I felt jaded, that I wanted to show Florida. But I couldn't do it."

In his freshman season, Doering worked with the scout team, but caught Spurrier's eye when he won the 12-minute run. Spurrier always preferred players who were in shape and did what they were told.

That year, Florida won its first-ever official SEC title and played in the Sugar Bowl. As a freshman walk-on, Doering flew out with the "hang-around guys" well after the team left for New Orleans.

"We didn't feel like we were part of the team," he said.

In 1992, Doering had moved up in the stretching line before practice. As a freshman, he said, he was so far in the back he was almost on the baseball field. But as a redshirt freshman, he made the travelling squad. At Tennessee in a 31-14 Vols win, Doering caught his first collegiate pass.

"Antwan Chiles threw me a curl," he said. "It hit my pads and popped up in the air but I caught it. I thought it was the greatest thing in the world."

As 1993 approached, Doering had moved into the top six at receiver. Florida was loaded at the position with Aubrey Hill, Jack Jackson, Willie Jackson, and Harrison Houston, so Doering knew his playing time was still in question.

Right before two-a-days, Spurrier announced to the team that Doering had earned a scholarship.

"I always felt lesser than the other guys because I didn't have a scholarship," he said. "It wasn't a financial thing because my parents could afford school. But to get it was validation from the coaching staff. I felt like I really earned it. If I had been one of those blue-chip guys, who knows if I would have worked as hard?"

Florida was coming off a difficult 1992 season. It was the last for record-setting quarterback Shane Matthews and he had been scrambling for his life behind a line that included two true freshmen at offensive tackles.

Still, the Gators had made the inaugural SEC title game, losing 28-21 to Alabama, and won the Gator Bowl over North Carolina State 27-10. There was optimism in the Gator camp even though they were breaking in a new quarterback in Terry Dean. There was still plenty of talent back, and Florida was ranked eighth in the preseason polls.

The big question was whether Dean could step into the role occupied by Matthews. *The Gainesville Sun*, in its college football special section, proclaimed on the cover, "It's Dean's Team."

Dean seemed perfect for the role, a strong-armed quarterback who had seen some time as Matthews' back-up. In Spurrier's system and with a better line, the offense was expected to continue to put up big numbers.

Chris Doering transformed from skinny soccer kid to a football hero for his beloved Gators. *The Gainesville Sun*

Florida fans were just settling into the Spurrier Era, thrilled that they had the SEC's best record in both 1990 and 1991 and flush with the belief another title was around the corner.

The Gators opened the season with an easy 44-6 win over Arkansas State and jumped a spot in the polls. Doering had caught a pair of passes and the Gators were prepared to travel to Lexington to face a Kentucky team they had beaten 35-19 in the '92 season opener.

"It just seemed like another week," Doering said. "We always beat those guys."

But it was different because Spurrier came up with a new slot formation that would include Doering, Houston, and Willie Jackson. Spurrier told the offense they would start the game with that formation.

Chris Doering was about to start his first college game.

"I was pumped," he said. "I remember thinking I've gone from walk-on to starter. I called my parents. They were going up for the game."

And what a game it turned out to be.

THE GAME OF MY LIFE
BY CHRIS DOERING

I always had a hard time sleeping before a game, but that Friday night was impossible. I took a football with me to Lexington, tossing it up in the air while I laid in bed and clutching it as I tried to get to sleep. Roommate Aubrey Hill and I discussed the differences between being a white player and a black player.

Finally, the morning of Game Day arrived. Even though the game was not televised, it started at 7:30 p.m. I hated night games.

Both the breakfast and pregame meal were a struggle. I always had to choke down food. The day of a game was always like that. But I had to eat because I knew I would need it. Always the same—spaghetti with no sauce because you'd burp that up, chicken, toast with jelly and a nutritional drink.

On the bus ride to the game, I had a routine of songs to play on my CD player, two from this CD, two from that, always in the same order. Someone took a picture of me on the field when we were walking around. I've got my headset on, just trying to get a feel for what was going to happen.

I remember Terry Dean tweaked his neck early while diving out of bounds and he was struggling. Coach Spurrier put Danny Wuerffel in, then back to Terry, then back to Danny. They ended up throwing seven interceptions.

Early in the fourth quarter, I made a diving catch in the end zone for a score. I was thinking that this was the greatest day of my life. At that point in my life it couldn't get any bigger.

But Kentucky had a long drive to get a field goal with under a minute to play to take a 20-17 lead. Harrison Houston returned the kickoff to put us in good shape and we drove it down to the Kentucky 28-yard line. Danny made the call—Steamers Y-7. I was the Y and would run a post.

I got held at the line and still almost made a one-handed catch. If I had caught it, we might have run out of time.

Back in the huddle, Danny called for the same play. Jack Jackson was wide right, and they thought it would go to him. They weren't worried about the skinny white dude. Both safeties went wide. There were eight seconds left in the game.

It's funny because when I was a kid watching Florida play, I was always nervous, and now watching Florida play, I'm nervous. But I was never nervous when I played. It was surreal.

I got a good release, and the guy covering me tried to run with me. The safeties were gone. You try to catch that ball 22 yards deep so you don't get hit by a safety. The ball seemed to be in the air forever. I caught it in the end zone and when I got to the fence a Kentucky fan took a swing at me.

Then I was mobbed by my teammates with all of those big linemen on top of me, I thought I was going to die. Their fans had been jawing at us all game on the sideline so I went back there and let them have it. I'm not proud of that.

I remember after the game thinking about all the times the Gators had a lost a game late and let me down. I had just saved a lot of people from being let down. That was a cool feeling.

THE AFTERMATH

Suddenly, Doering had turned from an afterthought to a hero. He was giving interviews after the game, right in the middle of the spotlight. In a physical education class the next week, the teacher was lecturing students about Chris Doering, not knowing he was in the class.

"It was a quick change going from somebody that nobody thought about to center stage," he said. "On Tuesday, we did the media day and Coach Spurrier told me to put that tape away and not watch it again. That was good because he was telling me not to settle on this one event.

"But still, to this day, when I meet someone they bring up that play. It's weird that the play you are remembered for happened early in your career."

In part, it was Mick Hubert's memorable call that immortalized the catch, "DOERING'S GOT A TOUCHDOWN! DOERING'S GOT A TOUCHDOWN!"

Florida went on to win the SEC that year, beating Alabama in the title game, and again the following season. In 1995, Doering's senior season, the Gators reached the national title game before losing to Nebraska. Doering was drafted in the sixth round by Jacksonville and spent the next nine years with five different NFL teams. In 2006, he put in his retirement papers with the NFL.

Doering lives in Gainesville with his wife, Tiffany, and two children. He does radio work and dabbles in different business ventures.

"I'm still looking for something that has the same passion as football," he said. "Football was my dream and it's hard to find something that gives you the same feeling."

Chapter 12

JIMMY DUNN

FLORIDA STATE AT FLORIDA
NOVEMBER 22, 1958
FLORIDA FIELD

PREGAME

Jimmy Dunn was born in Atlanta and grew up in housing projects at Clark Howell and Techwood near Georgia Tech. Those projects in downtown Atlanta were knocked down when the Summer Olympics visited the city in 1996.

He was a typical young boy, playing everything he could at playgrounds and the YMCA. It was a tough time for the Dunn family, but young Jimmy didn't know any better.

"My mother would yell at my father all the time that we had to get out of where we were living," he said. "I didn't know it was so bad because I didn't have anything to compare it to. I didn't know what existed two miles away. We were mobile, us kids, because we'd jump on the street cars and ride them. So we had some street sense."

When he was 13, the Dunn family moved to Tampa where Jimmy jumped right into the sports scene. Despite his lack of size, he found football to be his best sport.

"I always enjoyed football," he said. "I was never really good at anything but I could do a little bit of everything. There were guys who could throw it better, guys who could run inside better, guys who could

87

catch it better, guys who could punt it better. I could run, and I was a good listener."

At Hillsborough High, he played basketball, ran track, and was the quarterback on the football team.

"I tried to avoid confrontations," he said with a laugh. "It didn't bother me to run out of bounds. Later, when I was coaching, I would probably have said to me, 'How about getting an extra yard?'"

He was helped by a defensive scheme that required him as a safety to play 15 yards off the ball and keep the offense from getting big plays, which suited him fine.

In those days, a school from Tampa would have to travel to find big-time opponents so each year there would be trips to Miami, Jacksonville, Pensacola, and Orlando.

"We'd go back and forth on the train," he said. "Everything was first class. We stayed at hotels. It was like a small college. Now they never leave the county until they get into the playoffs."

Dunn's versatility got the attention of Tampa university coach Marcelo Huerta. Dunn knew everything about the school and was interested, especially since all of the other recruiters who came by would always say the same thing.

"You're too little to play," he said. "I would probably have said the same thing when I was coaching college football. It's one thing to see you on film and then they'd walk in the door and go, 'Dang, you need to be about 25 pounds heavier.' They all recommended I join the service and play there, get a little older and bigger and stronger."

But Tampa wanted Dunn, and he thought that might be the best place for him, playing in his hometown on a team he knew so much about.

But a visit to the school changed his mind.

"I was going to be the only freshman on scholarship and these guys were all married," he said. "They were mostly transfers who were older-looking, mature-looking guys who had wives and kids.

"I met a bunch of those guys and I couldn't see how I would fit into that group physically and mentally. These guys were 25, 26, and had been in the Korean conflict."

His wife-to-be was heading for Florida State, which, with the help of his high school coach, had shown an interest. FSU agreed to give Dunn

Jimmy Dunn's life has been immersed in football and continues to be so to this day. *University of Florida archives*

a one-year scholarship with the chance to go to spring practice and make the team.

"So I'm going to Tallahassee and Eleanor's there," he said.

But all of that changed on a summer day in Gainesville. Playing in the high school all-star game, Dunn put on a show. Competing against many players who were Florida signees, he won the Most Valuable Player honor, throwing a pair of touchdown passes and playing the whole game.

"I could see that I could play with those guys," Dunn said. "I could run with them. I understood the game. If they liked those guys, I knew I could play at the University of Florida. They could see I could play the game. I just wasn't 185 pounds, but I could do the same things they were doing."

Florida offered Dunn a four-year scholarship after the game. His family jumped at the idea, figuring that he could get his degree even though it was unlikely he would be a part of the football team for long.

For the Gator coaches, the job now was to put some weight on the freshman quarterback. The goal—15 new pounds by Christmas.

"The training table was the best food I've ever been a part of—quality and quantity," he said. "I did everything I could, three hot meals a day. On top of that, they worked out this deal where every night I'd go to the student cafeteria and they'd give me this milkshake. Plus, they were giving me weight-gain supplements.

"I'd go up there every night and get this milkshake made by the dietician that had everything in it, molasses and all of the old wives' tale things that were supposed to make you gain weight. Every night, seven days a week, before I went to bed. After a month, they weighed me and I was exactly the same weight. They said, that's enough of that."

He stayed at 142 pounds throughout his Florida career except for the 1957 season when he came down with the Asiatic flu and dropped five pounds.

On the practice field, the lithe freshman was watching the numbers dwindle. With almost 100 freshmen on the team and 100 other players, it was crowded until practice began heating up.

"The freshmen cut down quickly," Dunn said. "I'd see them leaving in the middle of the night."

Dunn played in three freshman games, but mostly was on the scout team where one week he was supposed to be Tennessee All-American Johnny Majors, running the single wing offense that was not that different from what a lot of college teams are running today.

Attrition moved Dunn up the depth chart as a sophomore. One quarterback quit, another was lost to grades. He made his first road trip to Starkville, Mississippi, for the opener and got into the game, driving his team to a touchdown in a 16-10 loss to the Bulldogs.

After a 1-1-1 start, the Florida coaches—who had brought Harry Spears back to school to be the quarterback—turned to Dunn, and the team won five games in a row, including a 28-0 thrashing of Georgia.

The following year, Dunn helped Florida to a 6-2-1 record that included a season-ending win at Miami, 14-0, and a national ranking. His senior season loomed with a team on the schedule for the first time—cross-state rival Florida State, the school he had turned his back on.

The state legislature got involved in the controversy over whether Florida and FSU should play, forcing the Gators to schedule the one-time girls school. As a result, it was a game circled on the calendars of both campuses.

But before that game would be played, Florida had eight to play. Losses to Mississippi State, LSU, and Auburn crippled the team's SEC hopes, but a 7-6 win over Georgia salvaged the season. In that game, Florida had no offense (zero first-half first downs) but Dunn broke an amazing 76-yard touchdown run—still the 12th longest in UF history—in the second half to win the game.

After an easy win over Arkansas State, the game was here—FSU coming to Gainesville for the first time.

THE GAME OF MY LIFE
BY JIMMY DUNN

Georgia was our biggest rival, but the FSU game in 1958 had such a big build-up. The legislature got involved and everybody, not just locally, was building the game up so much.

And then you had my relationship with FSU. They thought I was going there on the one-year deal but I decided to go to Florida. Their coach, Tom Nugent, was quoted as saying that I "lacked moral fiber."

Sure, I remembered that.

They had a good football team. They had beaten Tennessee in Knoxville so they weren't a bunch of rag-tags. We knew we were in for a tough game.

The thing is that if you're playing Auburn or Georgia Tech or Miami, you talk about it in the off-season, each one of them. But this off-season, all anybody was talking about was FSU, and it went on all year.

We kicked off to start the game, and they ran a double reverse. Bobby Renn took the ball and he was gone up the sidelines. He had a couple of blockers in front of him and I was the only one left. So I just started backpedaling. He ran to the middle of the field to try to outrun me but in the process he outran his blockers.

I saw what he was trying to do and was able to get him down. He panicked. He should have scored. If he had stayed with his blockers they'd have run over me.

But they punched it in later for a score and we knew we were in for a tough day. That's what got to us, that they ran this four-man I formation and just stuck it right into the end zone. We knew they were for real.

The whole game changed when Dave Hudson blocked a punt for a touchdown. They were leading and moving the ball on us. But that changed the whole game.

Vic Prinzi, their quarterback, got hurt and Joe Majors, who was Johnny's brother, came in. They still moved the ball but we kept them from scoring any more.

Twice we had fourth downs from their 10-yard line and their 12. Both times we called passing plays and both plays went exactly the same. They weren't designed runs, they were scrambles.

On both plays, I rolled to the right, couldn't find anyone open, and reversed my field to the left. I scored on both of them. And once we got ahead by two touchdowns, with Bobby Joe Greene punting, we knew it was over.

Lee Corso was the defensive backfield coach and he tells the story that if he wasn't such a good pass defense coach I'd have had to throw the ball, and I wasn't good enough to hit them so they'd have beaten us.

I also intercepted a pass in that game. What made it so great is that you played all the time so you had so many opportunities to make plays. It's funny, in 1957 I had six interceptions and nobody threw the ball. If I had played today, I might have had 20. Not really. It's a totally different game.

We won 21-7 and it was a great feeling. I was awarded the MVP for the game and I wondered what Tom Nugent was thinking. I didn't say anything but I knew it felt great.

It was a different game then. You had to play all of the special teams, covering punts when I wasn't punting, returning punts. There wasn't enough time in practice to put a lot in on offense so nobody played offense. It was defense and kicking.

I had some other big games, but that's the one that stands out. Everybody knew that we couldn't let them beat us, even though they brought their program along in such a short period of time. We couldn't let them, and there was a feeling of relief after the game.

THE AFTERMATH

Florida finished the regular season with a 12-9 win over Miami in Jacksonville and then lost 7-3 to Ole Miss in the Gator Bowl. Dunn was about to start a career as a coach.

He was hired by Ray Graves in 1960 to coach the B team and later coached defensive backs. He was hired by Doug Dickey at Tennessee in 1964—where Dunn was offensive coordinator and won two SEC titles—and returned to Florida when Dickey was named head coach in 1970.

When Dickey was fired in 1978, Dunn stayed at UF in a non-coaching position before starting a real estate company in Tampa. He returned to coaching as part of Steve Spurrier's staff with the USFL Tampa Bay Bandits in 1983.

After the league folded, Dunn worked as a scout for the Tampa Bay Bucs before entering the world of Arena Football in 1990. He also served as a head coach at various Arena II stops like Charleston, Myrtle Beach, and Corpus Christi, earning a reputation as being the man to get your franchise started.

Tired of the traveling, he returned to Tampa and worked with the Arena team there.

Dunn still lives in Tampa and is working with his former boss Doug Dickey on the new spring football league. He plans to coach in the league and still doesn't look like he could have ever played major college football.

Chapter 13

DON GAFFNEY

PREGAME

Don Gaffney was born in Jacksonville, Florida, one of five boys who all would go on to play college football. With five boys in the family, there were plenty of opportunities to play sports and plenty of chances to get into trouble.

But his was an upbringing of discipline and regimen.

"Things were different then," he said. "There was just a way you did things. You go to church on Sunday, you study, you're not going to get into trouble. You understand that you're going to work hard for anything you do. You go to school, do your chores. You leave the park, you come home, no detours.

"And if you get into trouble, you have to be man enough to deal with it."

Sports in the Riverside section of town was simply a bunch of kids getting together and playing in the streets or in the fields of Scott Park. There were no leagues for young black boys in Jacksonville in the '60s.

But when he was a pre-teen, then living on the north side of town, that changed.

"The Astro Gents Men's Club decided, 'We have to take some of these kids or we're going to lose them.' They created a league."

By then he had come under the tutelage, like many of the boys at Scott Park, of Denver Bronco Al Denson, a Jacksonville native who worked out in the off-season back home. Denson would sometimes bring Dallas Cowboy Bob Hayes, also a Jacksonville native, back to Scott Park for the workouts.

Gaffney would watch the workouts and mimic them when the pros were finished, But his football career got off to a slow start.

He didn't make the bantam football team as a 10-year-old, practiced every day but didn't dress out. A knee injury kept him out the next two years.

As a 13-year-old, he was among those who made up the last freshman class at Raines. But rather than play on a loaded junior high team, Gaffney took the advice of Earl Kitchens—the Raines coach and the father of one of Gaffney's best friends—to stay with the Astro Gents and get one good year of football in before tackling the next level.

"Raines was so loaded in football," Gaffney said. "They had Harold Carmichael and Truck Robinson playing quarterback. I'd be on the field with them and I could tell it wasn't my time. The quarterback at Raines had to be the best player on the field. They were all massive guys and they were all ahead of me."

But at 135 pounds, Gaffney was still good enough to win the Pop Warner championship and as a sophomore led his junior varsity team to an undefeated record in the Gateway Conference.

By the time he was ready to compete for the starting job as a junior at Raines, he had developed a strong arm despite his small physique.

"We would go home and we had a big yard," Gaffney said. "I'd throw to my brothers, Warren and Derrick, and other kids and we'd be doing the drills like we saw the pros do. My dad put up floodlights so we could play all night."

As a junior, Gaffney jumped ahead of two quarterbacks to be the starter at Raines. As a senior, the recruiters had become interested in

---

One of the best months in Florida football came in 1973 with Don Gaffney at quarterback—a "November to Remember."
University of Florida archives

Gaffney, but he wondered about the likelihood of a black quarterback playing in the South.

Doug Dickey was the Florida coach and spent plenty of time at Raines.

"He told my grandfather, 'I sure would like to see him throwing the ball in Gatorland,'" Gaffney said. "Tennessee was recruiting me real good. Kenny Lambert had played at Raines and was at Tennessee. He came back and told me how good the SEC was and that if Tennessee offered I had better take it. He told me they were going to start a black quarterback—Condredge Holloway. Eddie McAshan was at Georgia Tech and he was going to start. This was about the time Alabama got run over by Southern Cal and Bam Cunningham and they were starting to recruit black players. So things were changing."

On a visit to Florida, Gaffney sat in the press box and watched the junior varsity, led by quarterback David Bowden, play a game. The offense looked remarkably like the offense Gaffney was running at Raines.

And Gaffney had been a Gator fan all his life. Gainesville seemed so close to home, just down the road, and the other places seemed so far away. So he chose Florida and Dickey.

As a freshman at UF, Gaffney played in one freshman game but hurt his shoulder against Georgia. The next year, Bowden was the starter but Gaffney was able to get on the field.

"The most exciting game for me leading up to the Auburn game was at Death Valley (LSU)," he said. "We were behind and Coach Dickey told me at the half to stay loose because they might put me in there. I didn't really want that. We were behind, but this was David's team. Those were his boys.

"His class was real tight and we had come in with 12 black players and really hadn't bonded yet. And it was made more difficult with these experiments at quarterback. I didn't realize until I got there that quarterback at Florida is a sacred position."

Florida had started the 1973 season with high hopes and won its first two games over Kansas State and Southern Miss. The Gators were ranked 16th in the country when the wheels fell off.

They lost at Mississippi State and LSU and were trounced at home by third-ranked Alabama. Fans were growing restless with Bowden's erratic performances heading into a home game against Mississippi on Homecoming.

Gaffney expected to play in the game against the Rebels, but didn't take a snap.

"I had been playing well, but I think Coach Dickey was trying to instill some security in David," Gaffney said.

It didn't work out. Trailing 13-10 late in the game, Florida needed a first down to keep the last drive alive. Bowden thought a pass play had picked up a first down, but it had fallen a yard short. He rushed the team to the line and threw a pass out of bounds intentionally to stop the clock.

Except it was fourth down.

Florida's season was in shambles with a 2-4 record and a quarterback getting hammered by the fans and the press. There was an open date the following week before a game at Auburn, ranked 19th. To make matters worse, Florida had never won at Jordan-Hare Stadium.

THE GAME OF MY LIFE
BY DON GAFFNEY

Coach Dickey used to come into my room before games and we'd talk. I was kind of shy and he tried to bring stuff out of me. We were staying in Columbus, Georgia, and he came to my room the night before the game. Something was going on, I could tell.

We knew the situation we were dealing with. When I started getting snaps in practice, we knew something was happening.

I called my dad the night before the game and told him I didn't know what was going on, but I was getting a strange feeling. I was getting too many snaps in practice.

Sammy Green was my roommate and he told me, "Don, you have to be ready for this crowd." I was hearing all this and it was not registering.

The open week before the game on Wednesday we went into a mini-training camp and they switched the offense. We went to the veer with a sprint-out passing attack, anything to get me outside. We put so much of that stuff in, I knew they weren't putting it in for nothing.

They had put some other sophomores into the starting line-up, like Jimmy Dubose, but when we left Friday morning it was just normal. Nobody said anything to me. Jimmy Dunn was our offensive coordinator and he kept saying things to me about making sure I got my hands underneath center and the crowd noise, things he had never said before.

We warmed up, nothing was said. It was just normal. I had told my dad I might be starting, but if nothing else I was going to play a lot. He told me to just do my best.

We came back to the locker room after warm-ups and Coach Dickey walked up to me and handed me a football. "Don, you got it." You could hear a pin drop.

Wayne Fields, one of our defensive backs, said, "It's about time. This is what we've been waiting for." Nat Moore came over and said, "Gaff, go play your game. This is your time. Go play your game."

That's how much notice I had. And suddenly it hit me that they had switched the offense for me.

It was strange, though, because there wasn't much time to think. We had been talking about it, but I realized that this doesn't mean you are the man, it just means you can become the man because you're getting a chance.

More than anything, we needed the win. We needed it badly. I didn't even know that Florida had never won at Auburn. I didn't know the significance of it.

All I knew was that just like that we were on the field. They won the coin toss which was good for me because I could watch a few plays. But John Lacer forced a fumble and we got the ball in great field position.

We ended up missing a field goal on that first drive, but I knew my job wasn't to win the game, it was to not lose it. We had moved Vince Kendrick to tailback and Jimmy Dubose was inserted at fullback. My job was to let the running backs control the game, and get the ball to Joel Parker or Lee McGriff every once in a while.

The first pass I completed went to Joel for a touchdown. I was so well protected, it was just a matter of putting the football where it had to be. Coach (Jimmy) Dunn told me that the post pattern would work just like it was drawn up and it did.

We missed the extra point, but our defense was playing so well. I had only one check-off on offense. If they stacked to one side I called Yellow 33. But after a while, I noticed they were stacking to the other side so I told them I was going to switch the audible call. I called those two audibles six or seven times and they worked for big yardage.

Vince had 123 yards in the game, and in the third quarter he scored another touchdown. I ran a pitch play for the two-point conversion, but it wasn't there. We were up 12-0 and our defense wasn't about to see this get away.

But late in the game, I was running that same play I tried for the two-point conversion. I had the ball a little loose and got hit and fumbled. Auburn recovered.

I was devastated. They scored on the last play of the game and got the two-point conversion. I was crying. The defense played too well not to get a shutout. I was hurting. Those guys had played so well. The bottom line was that the score (12-8) didn't reflect the way we won the game.

So there we are winning for the first time ever at Jordan-Hare, and I was upset. It wasn't until after the game when the reporters were asking me about it that I understood. All of the great players who had been there, it was just our time.

I called my dad before we left Auburn and told him we were the first. You know what he said? "It was going to happen sometime." That was it.

I don't think I understood the significance of being the first black quarterback to start at Florida until after the next week when we beat Georgia. Once I'd started two straight games, a lot of reporters started asking me about it. I never thought of myself as a black quarterback. I knew that's what I was, but I just didn't think about it.

THE AFTERMATH

Florida had what was called a "November to Remember" as Gaffney led the Gators to wins over Georgia, Kentucky, Miami, and Florida State following the Auburn game.

The following year, he led his team to the Sugar Bowl and as a senior Florida lost only two regular-season games by a total of four points.

He played some semi-pro football with the Jacksonville Firebirds before finishing up his education. Recently, Gaffney was inducted into the Florida-Georgia Hall of Fame.

Gaffney lives in Jacksonville where he teaches law at Edward Waters College and an adjunct class at Florida Community College of Jacksonville.

He tries to stay involved in football and was the Pop Warner coach of NFL players Jabar Gaffney, his nephew, and Lito Sheppard.

Of the Gaffney brothers, Derrick made the biggest impact in the NFL, playing receiver for the New York Jets. But the Gaffney legacy at Florida is well established.

Chapter 14

BOB HEWKO

PREGAME

As a high school quarterback at Upper Moreland High in William Grove, Pennsylvania, Bob Hewko displayed a deft touch and a knack for playing several sports. The left-hander competed in basketball, baseball, and track but was recruited as a football player.

"I was probably better in baseball," he said. "I was a first baseman. But I gave up baseball my senior year to run track and work on my speed for football."

Hewko signed a letter of intent to play with Pittsburgh, but a Florida assistant coach named Steve Spurrier stopped by one of Hewko's basketball games to offer a trip to Gainesville.

Hewko fouled out of the basketball game, but the offer stood. He knew that Florida would be passing the ball with Spurrier working as a coach under Doug Dickey and was intrigued by the possibility of playing in the Sunshine State.

At the time, letters of intent were only binding within a conference, and Hewko was hooked as soon as he got off the plane in Florida.

"There was a Gator Getter there to meet me," he said. "She asked me if my name was Bob and I said it was and she told me she was my

103

host for the weekend. I don't remember her name but I remember what she looked like. She wasn't the only reason I decided on Florida, but she didn't hurt.

"I thought I was going to Pitt. My parents thought I was going to Pitt. I was the only guy they recruited that year out of eastern Pennsylvania. I just loved Florida when I visited, the school, everything. I remember (Pitt coach) Jackie Sherrill sitting in my living room for two hours after I signed with Florida. He couldn't believe I wasn't going to Pitt. But it worked out. If I had gone there, there never would have been a Dan Marino."

Hewko's brother Alex was on the football team at Florida and told his brother not to follow him to Gainesville because the Gators had signed an All-America quarterback named Cris Collinsworth.

But before Hewko returned to Pennsylvania, Dickey pulled him aside and said, "Cris Collinsworth is going to start for us somewhere, but it isn't going to be at quarterback."

Collinsworth went on to be an All-America wide receiver, catching passes from Hewko as a senior.

For Hewko, the climb to the starting job took some time. Dickey and Spurrier decided to redshirt most of the 1978 recruits. The following year, Hewko had to have knee surgery while his teammates were taking their lumps on the field. By then, Dickey had been fired and replaced by Pell.

"When they redshirted me my first year, I almost went back to Pitt," Hewko said. "I probably wouldn't have gone to Florida if I knew I was going to be redshirted."

But in 1980, Hewko took command of the job during spring practice. Mike Shanahan had been brought in as offensive coordinator and the two fit together perfectly.

After three straight wins to start the season, Hewko was hit by LSU's Ramsey Dardar while throwing a pass and suffered a torn medial collateral ligament in his right knee.

"My mom got the picture of it," he said. "I'm getting hit just as I'm releasing the ball. It's the same hit Carson Palmer took in the playoffs (in

---

Bob Hewko spent some time touring as a roadie with his friends in Mötley Crüe. *University of Florida archives*

2005). I was pretty depressed. We started out so fast and then my season was just over."

Peace took over as a true freshman and guided Florida to an 8-4 final record. The next year, Peace began the season as the starting quarterback. Hewko played well in some early games as a back-up and returned to the starting line-up only to suffer an injury to his left knee against Mississippi State. He did return and his touchdown pass in the Peach Bowl was the lone bright spot in a 26-6 loss.

The competition was open in 1982, but again a knee injury got in Hewko's way.

"I hurt it playing basketball with Tim Groves and Tyrone Young," he said. "But I was too afraid to tell the coaches so I told them I was running and I stepped in a hole."

Peace would be the starter with Hewko his back-up, coming into game to deliver a change of pace with his left-handed accuracy.

After two big wins over Miami and Southern Cal to start the season, Florida's season started to sink, finally hitting the bottom with a 44-0 loss against Georgia. After a pair of wins at Kentucky and Tulane, the Gators would finish the regular season against Florida State in Tallahassee—an unranked Florida at 15th-ranked FSU, where Florida had not won since 1976. Two years earlier, after a 17-13 loss at Doak Campbell, Charley Pell had told his team it would never again lose to the hated Seminoles. Florida had won 35-3 the following year in Gainesville, but winning on the road would be a tougher task.

THE GAME OF MY LIFE
BY BOB HEWKO

I think I helped my cause in that terrible loss to Georgia. Charley told me early in the season that any time Wayne screwed up, I was going in. But in that game, it was 44-0 with three minutes to go when he came to me and told me to go in. He said, "We need a drive." I mean, it was 44-0. I almost laughed when he said that.

When we got back to Gainesville, I went into his office. I wanted to know what the deal was. I told him, "I thought you were going to put me in the game when Wayne wasn't playing well and we're getting beat 44-0 before you put me in." He said, "You're right. You're absolutely right." So I think that helped when we played FSU.

Wayne started off slow and they got up on us 10-0. Coach Pell told me to get ready in the middle of the second quarter. It was raining pretty hard, but this was my last regular-season game and I wanted to have one last chance, especially against a team like Florida State. They were really good that year, really physical.

He put me in in the middle of the second quarter and we went right down the field. I was throwing to Dwayne Dixon and we had Lorenzo Hampton and James Jones and Neal Anderson. I knew we had to get something going against them and we did. I got into the huddle and said, "We need to go. We need to make something happen."

We got to their 9-yard line and it was second-and-goal. I looked over at Lee McGriff, who was the assistant signalling in the plays, and he was calling for an option play. Me? Run the option with my knees? I called time-out.

I went over to the sideline and Coach Shanahan was on the headset. He said that was the play they wanted. So we ran the counter option, and everyone on their defense went with James Jones. A nice little hole opened up and I just ran it. I like to say my great running ability got me in. I dove over some guy at the goal-line for the touchdown and now we had a game.

It was such a strange game, because Burt Reynolds was on the sidelines with some of his Hollywood friends and you'd look over and see him. And Bob Graham, who was the governor then, was working on the chain gang. It was one of his famous work days. You'd look over to get a play, and there was the governor working the chains.

It kept raining really hard, so there wasn't much offense. I didn't have a great game statistically (6-of-10 for 66 yards), but it was the kind of game where you'd get your butt kicked and then go back out and kick their butt the next play.

We got it tied up and had a late drive to try to win it. We got down to their 1-yard line and they called the option play again. But this time I got stood up really bad.

And then they called the play again. Mike Mularkey was our tight end and he looked at me and asked if I wanted to consider the pass option on the play. I didn't say anything. I just ran the play again and got stood up again.

As it turns out, I didn't look to the sidelines long enough. I saw what I thought was the same play but they were actually signalling in the pass option. I just didn't see it because I looked away before that part of the play came in.

So now it was fourth down and we called time-out. Coach Pell told me to take a delay penalty to give us a better angle on the field goal. So I took my time getting back to the huddle. The clock was running and our other tight end, Chris Faulkner, came running at me telling me to hurry up. I told him to chill out, that we were going to take the penalty.

We did, and Jim Gainey came in and kicked it through. There were about three minutes left and we stopped them to win it 13-10.

What happened next made this the game I'll always remember.

Coach Pell came up to me and hugged me and said it was the greatest game of his life. Later, he told the press that I would be sitting around telling my kids and grandkids about this game.

I was dating a cheerleader then and she came out at mid-field and gave me a kiss. Then, I grabbed the game ball and threw it into the end zone stands where all the Gator fans were sitting. I said later it was the best pass I threw all day.

Well, as soon as that ball landed in the stands, the Gator fans stormed the field. The cops were out there shooting tear gas and it was just crazy. The fans took down the goal post. I don't think the FSU people liked that very much.

It was such a fun game because it was raining, and they pretty much let me do what I wanted out there. When I went into the game, I asked for Chris Bromley to come in and be the center because it was so wet and we had a much better exchange because we worked together all week. So they sent him in and took John Redmond out. I know he wasn't thrilled.

It was so unexpected for us to win that game after getting beat so badly by Georgia. But that's what made it so much fun.

THE AFTERMATH

Hewko's final game as a Gator took place in Houston where he started against Arkansas in the Bluebonnet Bowl. Hewko played well, but Gary Anderson led the Razorbacks to a victory.

Peace went on to have a strong senior season for Florida, a 9-2-1 campaign that included a 53-14 thrashing of FSU in Gainesville.

Hewko went undrafted but signed a free agent contract with Tampa Bay. He also had brief stints with Dallas, the New York Giants, the Los

Angeles Rams, and Cleveland. Two more knee surgeries while he was with Tampa Bay ended any hopes of an NFL career, as he was out for his entire rookie season.

After leaving the NFL, Hewko was hired as the marketing director at Caesar's Palace in Las Vegas. He also had a stint as a part-owner and general manager of the Miami Hooters, an indoor football team from 1993-96.

Hewko now lives in South Florida and is licensed by 20 casinos in marketing for corporate events. He also served for several months as the road manager for Mötley Crüe.

Chapter 15

LINDY INFANTE

GEORGIA TECH AT FLORIDA
OCTOBER 1, 1960
FLORIDA FIELD

PREGAME

Growing up in sunny Miami, there was plenty of sports in Infante's young life. But it wasn't until junior high that football became a part of it.

"I was always athletic growing up," he said. "I had some friends at the Boys Club who said, 'Why don't you come play?' So I did play on the Boys Club little football team. We had a good team, a lot of good athletes. We won and had fun. I also played on the baseball team, and we traveled all over playing games."

Because there were only five high schools at the time in Dade County, the teams traveled north to play most of their games. Each year, Miami Senior High would play three teams in Jacksonville, making the trip by train. They also played a game each year in Key West.

"Back then, our home stadium was the Orange Bowl and we'd play in front of 35,000 or 40,000 people," Infante said. "It was a big-time deal. My senior year, there were 150 kids out for football. Luckily for me, as a junior I was starting on defense."

As a senior, Infante started his season out with a bang, scoring seven touchdowns in the first two games. But on a trip to Jacksonville, he suffered an injury and missed the middle of the season.

By then, Infante was playing exclusively as a running back. Even with the injury, letters came pouring in from colleges interested in signing him to a scholarship.

"Everybody recruited down there," he said. "For me, it came down to two schools—Florida and Georgia. I knew I wanted to live in Florida for the rest of my life so that was the deciding factor. And Hank Foldberg was recruiting me and he made me feel like I was very important to him. By the time he left the house, I wanted to know where to sign.

"Plus, I had friends who were going to Florida."

When he enrolled at Florida in 1959, freshmen were not eligible, so Infante played on the freshman team.

"We had a pretty talented team," he said. "I think that's one reason the 1960 team was so good. There were a lot of good players who came in as freshmen."

After a year on the freshman team, Infante stepped into the role of starter as a sophomore. By then, Florida had dumped Bob Woodruff as the coach and inserted Graves into the job.

"It wasn't a huge deal to me because when you were a freshman, you didn't really see the head coach until after practice," he said. "Back then, the freshmen would come out after practice and plug the field. We'd walk through the practice field replacing the divots that had been taken up, just walk along in a line replacing the plugs, stomp them back in.

"Freshmen were basically cannon fodder for the varsity to beat on. I was recruited under Coach Woodruff's watch, but I never knew the man. We had our own coaches. We did our own thing. We did what the varsity told us to do and played our own four games against other freshman teams."

Florida started the Graves Era by beating George Washington 30-7. A week later, the Gators nipped Florida State 3-0 in only the third game ever played between the two schools.

That set up a monumental game against Georgia Tech the following week.

Lindy Infante was one of the most accessible and likable coaches for writers to deal with in the NFL and USFL. *University of Florida archives*

The Yellow Jackets were one of the power teams in college football. They were ranked 10th in the nation coming in. Florida was not ranked.

But it was a big game because it would be the first real big test for Graves in his first year on the job.

THE GAME OF MY LIFE
BY LINDY INFANTE

The thing that made the game special was the backdrop.

Ray Graves had come to us from Georgia Tech. It was his first year. Bobby Dodd was the coach at Tech and they were a real powerhouse back in those days. And Bobby Dodd Jr. was our passing quarterback, so there was a lot of talk about who Mrs. Dodd would be rooting for.

It was Tech vs. Florida, Dodd vs. Graves, Dodd vs. his son.

It was an interesting game. It was nip and tuck all the way. They would fumble, we'd fumble it right back. The amazing thing was, looking back, they punted on third down three times, and one time they quick-kicked on second down. It was a different game then, all about field position and defense and turnovers.

They were all about pinning us back and trying to force a mistake. I played both ways and I actually had eight tackles and only six carries in the game. You stayed on the field until they dragged you off.

We backed them up and they punted on a third-and-5. They just wanted to get off that end of the field. We played the first quarter at their end of the field.

In the second quarter, they quick-kicked down to our 13 on one play. That set up an opportunity for them to get a short field and a drive going but they fumbled at our six. We got the ball back and fumbled at the 26 and they took it in and finally scored.

Then they fumbled at their 23 and Don Deal scored on a pitch-out from Larry Libertore, our quarterback. Dodd Jr. was our passer, and Larry was the running quarterback.

Then they got a drive going passing the ball seven times and got a field goal out of it. So it was 10-7 at the half.

In the second half, Jon MacBeth intercepted a pass at our 11. Later, they punted on third down and shanked it out of bounds at the 37 and we got a field goal out of that to make it 10-10. It was just a back-and-forth kind of game.

They drove 73 yards for a touchdown to make it 17-10 and we came right back with a 14-play drive at the end of the third quarter and beginning of the fourth, but we missed a field goal.

So after all of that, we got the ball at our own 15 and we knew it was the last drive of the game. That is where the game was made.

We put together a 17-play drive, 85 yards. Early in the drive, we had a second-and-20, got a couple, and had a third-and-18, but we got the first down.

So we drove it down to the two, first down. We got one yard, then Don Goodman got half a yard. It was third down and Bobby Dodd Jr. muffed a snap and recovered it back at the four. So it was fourth down, game on the line.

The call was to run a little option play to the right. Libertore was the quarterback and I knew in that kind of situation he liked to fake the pitch and dart up in there, keeping the ball. I was trailing him and I figured he'd just keep it.

Well, he faked the pitch once and they corralled him. So he flipped it out to me and kind of caught me by surprise.

I controlled the ball and barely snuck in inside the pylon. We had a picture in my house here in Crescent Beach that we don't have anymore because it was water damaged by one of the hurricanes. It showed me diving into the corner and in the background there were 33 seconds left. I always thought that was neat because that was my number.

The crowd was going crazy. They were all chanting for us to go for two. I don't know how much that played into Coach Graves' decision, but he stuck the two fingers up, which is now the famous photograph.

The play was a play-action pass, and I was one of the options. But MacBeth opened up and Libertore again faked like he was going to run it and hit him open in the end zone to make it 18-17.

They got the ball back but we intercepted it and that was the game.

When you are part of a game like that, it's exhilarating. We were all excited. For me, scoring that last touchdown, it was even more exciting. It was such a dramatic game because the game had gone back and forth all day.

I remember I went back to my room. We were all going to go out and celebrate. I was on the second floor at Yon Hall and started down the stairs. But I cramped up all over. Two guys next door picked me up and took me back to my room. I waited about an hour for the cramps to go away and then we went out and celebrated a great victory. It was a very sweet win for us.

THE AFTERMATH

Florida was ranked 18th the following week, but lost 10-0 to Rice in Miami. But the Gators recovered to beat LSU, Georgia, and Miami before edging Baylor in the Gator Bowl 13-12 to complete the first nine-win season in Florida history.

Infante played both ways again as a junior, but the Gators struggled to a 4-5-1 record. By the time he was a senior, LSU had introduced platoon football to the game with its Chinese Bandits.

"Our starters played both ways to start a game, but midway through we had a blue team that would come in," Infante said.

But the platoon system couldn't save Infante from injuries. In a 23-0 loss at LSU, Infante suffered a broken nose and broken ankle. He didn't play the rest of the season.

"Same game, different plays," he said.

Infante was drafted by both the NFL Cleveland Browns and AFL Buffalo Bills. He chose Buffalo, which put him at wide receiver. A broken toe led to him being one of the last players cut and he went to Hamilton of the CFL for a few games.

"They wanted me back the next year but I decided to find out what was going to be my life's work," he said.

His plan was to be an architect, but while interning at Miami Edison to finish up his degree in education, Infante was asked to help coach the football team. The following year, Miami Senior hired him to be the backfield coach and the team went 12-0.

"I decided I'll be poor all my life, but I wanted to coach," he said.

He was hired at Florida as a graduate assistant, then took over the freshman team. It was the beginning of a decorated career as a coach in the USFL, where he was the head coach of the Jacksonville Bulls, and in the NFL.

Infante coached at Tulane twice and a Memphis State. He was the head coach in Jacksonville of the USFL in 1984 and 1985. And he also had a stint in the World Football League in Charlotte in 1975.

But it was in the NFL that Infante gained the most fame. He coached as an assistant with the New York Giants starting in 1977 before moving to Cincinnati in 1980. After two seasons as quarterbacks coach, he was named offensive coordinator following the 1981 season. From there it was off to the USFL, but he was back to the NFL as offensive coordinator in Cleveland after the USFL folded.

In 1988 he was named the head coach of the Green Bay Packers and lasted four seasons. In 1989, he was named NFL coach of the year, but in the NFL you are only as good as your last season, and he was let go after the 1991 season.

Infante ended up in Indianapolis as an offensive coordinator and was named head coach there in 1996 and '97, getting the Colts to the playoffs in '96.

But after being let go following the '97 season, Infante took his settlement and basically retired, although he has coached in some all-star games.

One bit of irony—had Steve Spurrier left after Florida's 1995 season and moved to the NFL to coach the Tampa Bay Bucs, Infante likely would have been the coach to replace him as the Gators head man.

Infante has always had a love affair with Crescent Beach, the beach town just south of St. Augustine where Spurrier, Bobby Stoops, and Billy Donovan all have summer homes. Infante's is right on the ocean and he has spent the years after his retirement wind-surfing and playing golf.

He lives in the house with his wife, Stephanie, and recently built a pool for his grandchildren. He still keeps track of his old college team.

Chapter 16

TAYLOR JACOBS

PREGAME

Born in Tallahassee, Taylor Jacobs was active as a child participating in the usual sports—football, basketball, baseball, and soccer. In his younger days, he was an excellent soccer and baseball player, but football was his real passion.

From tee-ball to flag football to soccer to pick-up basketball games, sports were a year-round thing for Jacobs.

But when he was 12, his father put an end to his soccer career.

"Once I was heading to high school, he wanted me to quit playing soccer because there was no real future in it," Jacobs said. "He wanted me to play football."

But as a smallish football player, he found it difficult to get on the field as a freshman at FAMU High School. He kicked as a freshman before a growth spurt allowed him to play quarterback.

But that didn't work out either.

"We ran a wishbone offense, so all I did was hand the ball off and hardly ever just dropped back," he said. "My dad was the coach so there was extreme pressure on me from everybody else. It was not fun. I really believed it was messing with my confidence."

Jacobs even transferred to Florida High just to get away from the pressure. He lasted one day before returning to FAMU High.

There he was becoming a star on the baseball field, playing shortstop and center field. He also was the team's closer on the mound.

"I could really bring it," he said. "But I was only good for two or three innings."

He went to summer football camps at Florida State and Auburn as well as Florida trying to hone his football skills.

"It got me some exposure," he said. "And I wanted to find out what kind of university I wanted to attend."

Despite being a high school All-American at wide receiver in his senior year, both Florida and FSU were leery of his lean frame and wanted him to walk on.

"But we couldn't afford for me to go to one of those schools without a scholarship," he said.

He had played several positions that senior year, but Florida had already received commitments from Jabar Gaffney and Elgin Hicks. Finally, Steve Spurrier showed up in Tallahassee for a visit and took a chance on Jacobs, offering him a scholarship.

"The problem was that I had never been exposed to a weight room," he said. "When I was at Florida, I gained 22 pounds."

With his speed and an offense that often went to four and five wide receivers, Jacobs found himself playing as a true freshman for the Gators in 1999. Florida had Travis Taylor and Darrell Jackson, among others, so even though he was playing, Jacobs caught only three passes.

The following season, he was slightly more involved, but was under the radar in Spurrier's explosive offense. The Gators won the SEC that year, but Jacobs was still trying to find himself.

"I wasn't doing the things I was supposed to do," he said. "It wasn't my time. But Buddy Teevens, who wasn't my position coach because he coached the running backs, really helped me. He was a real positive person in my life. I thank him for what he did for me.

"I had caught a long pass against FSU as a freshman on a play they put in just for me. But 2000 was the worst year for me. My back was against the wall after that season. I couldn't have done much worse."

To make it even more difficult, Florida signed five receivers in the Class of 2001—Carlos Perez, O.J. Small, Kelvin Kight, Reggie Vickers, and Matt Jackson. Vickers was a bust, and Jackson moved to defensive back, but the other three had productive careers at Florida.

"I knew Coach Spurrier wanted good things for me, but I had no faith right then," Jacobs said. "I just didn't think anyone would do anything special for me. But I finally decided that there was only one way to go and that was to go all out or don't go at all. At the end of the day, if it wasn't good enough, screw it.

"I was going to do my best and see what happened, just try to clear my mind as much as possible and go out and perform."

On the practice field in spring practice before his junior season, Jacobs was a star. He kept getting behind the secondary and caught seven touchdown passes in scrimmages.

Still, Florida had plenty of firepower in 2001 other than Jacobs. With Rex Grossman winning the job in the summer from Brock Berlin, the Gator offense rolled into the season with a pair of star wide receivers in Gaffney and Reche Caldwell.

Jacobs was the third receiver and made the most of his limited opportunities. He caught 38 passes during the season, and seven of them went for touchdowns.

For the team, it was a strange season. September 11 forced the Gators and every other team in college football to postpone their games in the third week of the season. The annual big game with Tennessee would be moved to the end of the season.

Florida rolled through the first half of the season and Grossman set the all-time record for passing yards in a game at LSU. But on a windy night in Auburn, the Gators lost at Auburn as Grossman struggled without running back Earnest Graham.

As a result, after a win against FSU, Florida went into the season-ending game with the Vols with so much on the line. A win would put them in the SEC Championship Game and the Rose Bowl was a real possibility.

But in the FSU game, Graham suffered a knee injury. Spurrier felt that Graham was intentionally injured by FSU defender Darnell Dockett and complained loudly throughout the week.

It wasn't Spurrier's offense that failed against the Vols, but a defense that couldn't stop Travis Stephens. A late score was followed by a missed two-point conversion and Florida lost 34-32.

The first play of the Ron Zook Era at Florida was a deep pass from Rex Grossman to Taylor Jacobs. *The Gainesville Sun*

No SEC title game, no Rose Bowl. Just a lot of disappointment in the Gator Nation.

Still, there would be a BCS bowl game for Florida—the Orange Bowl against ACC champion Maryland. It was a nice consolation prize for a team that was loaded with talent and lost two games by a total of five points.

THE GAME OF MY LIFE
BY TAYLOR JACOBS

It was a weird week leading up to the game because Rex was suspended for the start of it. It was difficult because Rex was our leader. But we also knew that Brock Berlin was a great quarterback. He had a lot of talent. They had been fighting for the starting job in the preseason. Now it was Brock's turn. That was our attitude.

It was just Rex being Rex. He was the best passer I ever saw.

Before the game, Coach Spurrier told me, "You're going to get an opportunity to do some things in this game." I just tried to prepare myself to do what I did every game—just don't worry about "what if something bad happens."

But I had no idea it would be a night to remember; a night I'd never forget.

Early in the game I caught a long touchdown pass, a 46-yarder from Brock that put us up 14-0. It was a feeling that is hard to describe, to catch a long touchdown pass in a game like that. It's close to a numb feeling. You don't realize what is happening.

As the game went on, you don't realize how big it was what you're doing. You don't realize what you've done.

You're put out there to make plays and that's what you have to do. But I was the third receiver. so you don't think it's going to be a night like it turned out to be.

Brock struggled a little, threw a couple of interceptions, and Rex came in about halfway through the second quarter with us ahead 14-10. Rex was on fire. He drove us to touchdown after touchdown. I played hard for both of them.

The balls just kept coming to me. I definitely didn't see it coming, since I wasn't used to being in the spotlight. I just kept making catches and I was thinking, "Is this really happening to me?"

I ended up catching 10 passes for 170 yards and another touchdown pass, a 15-yarder from Rex. I had never had a game like that. It wasn't until a few days later that I really understood how big a deal it was.

But Coach Spurrier had a bunch of big plays ready. He always did, so I thought I could get some, especially after he told me that some of those plays could come to me.

It was amazing. I was up there on the stage after the game with Coach Spurrier, and he said that he had told me some balls were going to come to me. They gave me the MVP trophy and it was filled with oranges. It's sitting on top of my television at home in Tallahassee, but without the oranges.

Coach Spurrier asked me if I was going to throw some of those oranges up in the stands. It was amazing. I was still thinking, "This can't be happening to me."

I got a bunch of calls from people who didn't think I had it in me. It was a crazy time. I hadn't even thought about coming out early before the game and now people were asking me if I was going to come out. It was wild.

I remember thinking that it couldn't get any better than this. And then, a couple of days after the game, Coach Spurrier announced that he was leaving Florida for the NFL. I didn't know what to think.

THE AFTERMATH

Once Ron Zook was hired to replace Spurrier at Florida, Jacobs and Grossman both had decisions to make. That decision came at a restaurant in Gainesville where the two met with their families for dinner.

Grossman shook Jacobs' hand and told the receiver that they both should stay for another year.

"Rex was a big factor in that," Jacobs said. "He told me, 'We're going to do some great things together.' So we decided together to come back for another year. Rex was going to be a top-20 pick and thought he could be a top-five pick with another year. I thought I could rise in the draft, too, if I came back."

Jacobs' senior season was an extension of his Orange Bowl. He became Grossman's favorite target and had a big year, the kind of year he always hoped to have at Florida.

But the Gators struggled, going 8-5 and losing in the Outback Bowl. Jacobs had improved his draft status with a 71-catch season and waited for the draft.

He was selected in the second round ... by Spurrier. The former UF coach had taken the job as head coach in Washington and wanted to load up his team with players from Florida who knew his system.

But for Jacobs, his rookie year was riddled by injuries. He caught only three passes for 37 yards. The next season with the Redskins, he caught 16 passes for 178 yards. Spurrier left the NFL after those two seasons, upset with the lack of control he had in Washington.

Jacobs remained in Washington for another season where he caught 11 passes for 100 yards. He was traded to San Francisco where injuries were again an issue. Jacobs caught four passes for the 49ers in 2006.

Jacobs lives in Tallahassee in the off-season and will be with San Francisco again in 2007, still looking for that breakout season in the NFL.

Chapter 17

JAMES JONES

PREGAME

Jones was one of those do-everything players at Pompano Ely High, an athlete with size, speed, and a high football I.Q. who could play almost every position. After a game in his sophomore season of high school, the Fort Lauderdale *Sun-Sentinel* ran a feature story on him with the headline, "The Franchise."

"I never came off the field," he said. "I was kind of all over the place. We had a coach who made sure you were in shape and you didn't want to leave the field. Playing high school ball, you had no worries.

"It really helped me that I had three older brothers who were really good athletes and kind of paved the way for me. They all went on to play college football as well."

He played quarterback, fullback, wide receiver, linebacker, and defensive line for Ely and even did a little placekicking. He returned kicks as well and helped Ely win its district title in his senior year.

As a result, Jones was one of the most coveted players in the 1979 recruiting class. He had his choice of colleges.

"I could have gone anywhere," he said. "Alabama, Penn State, Georgia Tech, UCLA, Florida State, Miami. They were all recruiting me heavily. But everyone wanted me to play running back. I wanted to play tight end.

"That was the position I was really in love with. I'd watched Kellen Winslow play for the Chargers and I always thought that was what I wanted to be. I didn't mind blocking. I liked playing tight end."

Jones finally settled on Florida because Charley Pell, the UF coach at the time, promised Jones he could play tight end.

"That was part of it, that he promised me a chance," Jones said. "But it was more than that. I wanted to go to school in a state where I was going to live the rest of my life. I knew it would help business-wise. It's all about—the way I grew up and learned—that eventually you were going to be networking and it mattered where you went to school. Believe me, it has helped being a University of Florida graduate."

Jones arrived on campus a 210-pound tight end and went to work to add weight to his frame. By the time the 1979 season started, he was up to 225 pounds.

He was also a starter as a true freshman at tight end as the Pell Era began against Houston.

"That was the only game where I was nervous the night before," he said. "Usually I just relaxed the night before a game, but I was nervous that night. Houston was ranked (13th) and we were such a young team. It was a shock when I got out there. It was definitely a different level. But I held my own."

Florida lost that game in Houston 14-10, the first of 10 losses in an 0-10-1 season. Jones started five games, played in them all, and had to deal with the taste of defeat far too often.

"It was hard," he said. "People think we were lousy, but we were in a lot of close games. Just a bounce here or there and we'd have won a few. But the year before, we had won the district championship, so I wasn't used to losing."

As he hit the practice field the following spring, Pell delivered the news to Jones that he would be moving to fullback.

"That was fine with me because we had tight ends coming in and Chris Faulkner and Mike Mularkey were there, but we didn't have many

---

James Jones was the color commentator on radio when Florida won its first national title in 1996. *University of Florida archives*

running backs or fullbacks," Jones said. "The position was wide open. I felt like it was a good move for me.

"And I was used to having the ball in my hands a lot in high school. There were times when I wondered if I made the right decision with the school I picked. Every player—whether he's at Florida or FSU or Miami—has those little doubts cross his mind. But I don't think you can ever make a bad decision. It is what it is."

As a sophomore, Jones led the team in rushing with 657 yards, averaging 4.4 yards a carry. The Gator offense under offensive coordinator Mike Shanahan was spreading the field and throwing a lot of passes in the four-receiver offense. Often, Jones was the only back in the backfield.

Florida turned it around to go 8-4 that year, but lost its last two regular-season games to Miami and Florida State.

The following year, Jones again led the team in rushing with 617 yards and scored nine touchdowns. But tough losses to Miami, Auburn, and Georgia and an embarrassing final game loss to West Virginia in the Peach Bowl put a damper on another winning season.

Heading into the 1982 season, Florida was considered to be a team on the rise. Pell was in his fourth year and seemed to have all of the ingredients in place to make a run at Florida's first-ever SEC title.

"He was a great coach to play for," Jones said. "He got you motivated. He surrounded himself with great assistant coaches, which always makes the coach's job easier. He treated me with a lot of respect. I still look up to him even though he has passed away and I have a lot of respect for his wife and family."

With a team loaded with veterans, expectations were high in Gainesville. Florida started the season ranked 16th, had a pair of veteran quarterbacks in Wayne Peace and Bob Hewko, seniors along the offensive line and a defense that was fast and aggressive.

But to start the season, the Gators would have to get past a rival that had their number. Miami had won four straight over Florida, and in its last trip to Gainesville had pasted the Gators 31-7.

The year before, the Hurricanes had opened the season by beating UF 21-20 on a late field goal by Dan Miller from 54 yards out.

"We felt like we were looking at big things," Jones said. "We had a lot of leaders on the team. As a senior, I was one of them. We wanted to show that we were one of the elite teams in the country."

THE GAME OF MY LIFE
BY JAMES JONES

All that week there was a lot of trash-talking, which was typical. That's part of a rivalry. You knew it was going to be a tough game. We felt like we had everything in place, but so did Miami. They had Jim Kelly and a great defense. So you went in knowing it was probably going to be a low-scoring game.

Practices were tough that week but that wasn't unusual under Coach Pell. There were times when we'd practice for 13 periods and he'd go, "Grrr. Let's go back and start over at the first period." And we would have already been out there for 45 minutes. Start over. But it was our fault. We were the ones who weren't practicing right.

The night before the game I was pretty relaxed like I always was. We knew it would be a tough game but we were glad to be playing them in Gainesville. It was a little tight around our team because we hadn't beaten Miami in a while. I'm pretty sure Coach Pell was uptight, too. The pressure was on him as well because Miami had beaten us four years in a row.

We got to the stadium and they had just put in a new part of the stadium, the south end zone. We wanted to christen it the right way. But we knew it was not going to be easy.

They had a really tough defense. And it was hot. We were playing on that astroturf and the heat index was 140 degrees. But we were used to practicing in the heat and so was Miami, so that didn't have anything to do with the game.

Both sides were playing great defense. We moved the ball OK in the first half. I ran a few off tackle and a couple of draws, caught two or three passes. We scored and they scored. They made some adjustments for the second half and we had trouble moving the ball.

Our spread offense worked against some teams, but Miami had so much speed and quickness. They ran down our guys and we were having trouble doing a whole lot in the second half on offense. But our defense was playing well.

They went down and scored late in the game to take a 14-10 lead. Wayne Peace was the leader of our offense, and he pretty much took over. Plus, we had a whole bunch of older guys—Mularkey and Dan Fike and Spencer Jackson. It was a senior team and we felt confident in the huddle.

Wayne moved us down the field, but they were shutting me down for the most part and our tailbacks weren't there yet. We got down to the 18-yard line, and Wayne called a naked bootleg play. We had run it earlier in the game and he hit the tight end for a touchdown.

On that play, he fakes to me and then to the tailback and he has two options, the tight end dragging across the field or me in the flat. They stayed on the tight end this time and everyone else went with (wide receiver) Dwayne Dixon. I was wide open in the flat, but Wayne didn't throw it to me. I was thinking, "What are you doing? I'm wide open." Nobody came with me.

If he had thrown it then, I might not have scored. The defense would have reacted and, who knows, I might have broken a tackle and gotten in, but there certainly is the possibility I wouldn't have gotten in, and who knows what night have happened?

Finally, after looking for the other guys, Wayne saw me downfield still wide open. It was like, "Oh, there he is." He was about to get sacked and threw a floater off his back foot. It was like playing baseball, and you think you've come in too far for the ball. I thought it was going to go over my head. I started back-pedaling and just stretched for it.

It hit my right hand and palm perfectly and I pulled it in and floated through the air for a couple of yards. The official signalled touchdown and Mularkey and Dwayne jumped on me. It was a great feeling. You don't realize the magnitude of something like that at the time it happens, but as time goes by it means a lot.

You look at it now, the pictures of the catch, and it does look like I was down just before the end zone. But I've told Jim Kelly that if they had marked me down at the 1-yard line we would have run more time off the clock and not given them 1:18 to come back and try to score. He's never really bought into that.

Our defense stopped them cold and we won. It was an unbelievable feeling. I still have the picture from *Sport Illustrated* and I send it to almuni from time to time when I want to do business with them.

THE AFTERMATH

The play became known simply as "The Catch" and helped propel UF to an eventual No. 4 ranking. But the season ended up like so many others when losses to LSU, Vanderbilt, and Georgia derailed any hopes of an SEC title for the Gators.

Jones went on to be the 13th pick of the Detroit Lions in the 1983 NFL Draft and had seven productive seasons with Detroit. He was traded to Seattle where he played four more years before returning to Detroit. A torn stomach muscle put Jones on the injured reserve list for the entire 1993 season, and he retired when it was completed.

When his NFL career was over, Jones had rushed for 3,626 yards and 26 touchdowns. He also caught 318 passes for 2,641 yards and 10 more touchdowns.

Jones lived in Detroit before moving to Tampa in 1996.

Jones set up shop in Tampa and still lives there. He works for Brown and Brown Insurance and also has done work with the Gator Radio Network, serving as color analyst for several years and now as one the pre-game hosts.

He also is coaching his sons in high school.

"One's a linebacker, the other's a safety," he said. "But they could play fullback if they had to."

Chapter 18

CHRIS LEAK

FLORIDA VS. OHIO STATE
JANUARY 8, 2007
UNIVERSITY OF PHOENIX STADIUM
GLENDALE, ARIZONA

PREGAME

Chris Leak was born in Charlotte, North Carolina, and was immersed in the culture of football at an early age. His father, Curtis, played in the NFL for Green Bay and his brother C.J. also played quarterback.

As a young boy, he followed C.J. everywhere and was even the mascot for the team his brother quarterbacked in the Charlotte Youth Football League, which was started by his father.

"I never played other sports," Leak said. "I don't know why. My father tried to get me to play basketball in high school, but I just wanted to play football, and I wanted to be a quarterback. I was the mascot until I was old enough to play when I turned eight.

"I tagged along with C.J. everywhere, and I think that's why I wanted to be a quarterback, because he was a quarterback. Everyone used to call me 'Little C.J.' but I didn't mind. I liked being compared to my brother. That was great for me. I never looked at it as being in the shadow. I'm proud of things my big brother did. I copied everything he did, and I think that's why it came naturally to me."

Leak played in the CYFL until he was 13 years old. By then, he already had a scholarship offer.

It was national news when Wake Forest, where C.J. would start his college career, offered Leak a scholarship before before he was in the eighth grade.

"My dad, who loved to coach, coached both us us in the CYFL," Leak said. "He took us to five or six summer camps at different schools. Jim Caldwell was the coach at Wake Forest and he saw that I could play, so he offered me a scholarship.

"I didn't even know what a scholarship was. But I committed to Wake because my brother was there."

In the CYFL, he played quarterback and strong safety.

"I used to try to clean people out, try to get a full head of steam, and go after them on defense," he said.

By the time he started high school at Charlotte Independence, he was a full-time quarterback. Leak earned the starting job from the first game of his freshman year and was the team's quarterback throughout high school.

After his freshman year, Tom Knotts moved to Independence as the head coach from crosstown rival West Charlotte.

"My first year, we threw some, but we ran more option," Leak said. "Coach Knotts came in and he loved to throw the football."

As a senior, Leak led his team to a perfect record and a state championship. By then, Caldwell had been fired at Wake Forest, and C.J. had moved to Tennessee.

Leak assumed he would follow his brother to Rocky Top. But everything changed on a fateful day in Athens, Georgia. C.J. got his first start but was pulled after two series. Both Chris and Curtis were watching in the stands.

"I was big on Tennessee, but I was keeping my doors open to other schools," Leak said. "They ran the ball six times and he got pulled. After seeing what he went through, Tennessee was out of the picture."

Leak took visits to five schools—Florida, Florida State, Southern Cal, Iowa, and Texas. The recruiting process was difficult, and Curtis Leak installed a special phone line for coaches to call to keep it as manageable as possible.

Leak was also chronicling his thoughts for a weekly feature on ESPN.com.

"The recruiting process was tough," Leak said. "My dad would have to rush home from work to make sure he was there for the coaches' visits. One day, we had three different coaches come to the house."

The winner was Ron Zook at Florida. He wrote a detailed letter the Leaks explaining his plan for the advancement of the young quarterback's career. That was the clincher.

"He broke down the plan for me, how he was going to get me to ready to play," Leak said. "Not every coach did that. That showed me something about Coach Zook."

The day before the U.S. Army All-Star game after his senior year, Leak made up his mind. On national television, he put on a Gator cap.

With Rex Grossman leaving a year early for the NFL, Leak would compete with Ingle Martin, Gavin Dickey, and Justin Midgett for the starting job in Zook's second season. Martin started the season, but Leak took over the job after four games.

His first start was almost a disaster. Trailing at Kentucky 21-3, Leak rallied the Gators to a 24-21 victory. He also engineered a stunning win over LSU, which went on to win the national championship.

As a sophomore, with Martin transferring, Leak was the clear starter. Midway through the season, after a loss to Mississippi State, Zook was told he was fired, effective at the end of the season.

"It was very emotional for everyone," Leak said. "Coach Zook had such a great relationship with me. I still call him all the time. He had great relationships with everyone. But I don't think it really hit me until the bowl game (which Zook did not coach) and he wasn't there."

Enter Urban Meyer. One of the first things Meyer did when he took the Florida job was to call his quarterback. Leak was in Atlanta for the SEC Championship Game between Tennessee and Auburn, there to support his brother.

"I was at the hotel when he called and the first question was, 'Are you ready to go to work?'" he said. "So I knew I had a coach who wanted to work with me and make me a better player. That gave me a lot of confidence."

Florida went 9-3 in Meyer's first season, but the offense that had been so effective when Leak had led the SEC in passing in 2004 sputtered at times. Losses at Alabama, LSU, and South Carolina meant Leak would enter his senior season without any championship rings.

He also had to adjust to his third offensive coordinator in three years and an offense that was not only designed for a more mobile quarterback but an offense that was without some of its biggest playmakers much of the season.

"The first year of an offense, you can't go full speed because you're thinking all the time," Leak said. "A lot went on that first year with Coach Meyer.

"It was the next spring when, for me, it clicked. I went to the coaches and told them I want to do a bunch of check-with-me plays at the line. That's what we did in 2006. I'd go to the line with a play, but with three other alert plays, like Peyton Manning does. Until Coach Meyer came in, our center Mike Degory called all of the protections.

"I learned so much about the running game and getting the right protections. With Coach Meyer, everything is about the quarterback knowing everything."

Even with Florida winning in 2006, there was plenty of criticism for the senior quarterback. And there was the adjustment of a freshman quarterback coming into the games on short yardage plays.

Leak never flinched, even when some Florida fans booed when he was put back into the game against Kentucky at home after Tim Tebow drove the Gators down the field.

"I never paid attention to it," Leak said. "The people I paid attention to were my dad, my brother (who had joined the Florida staff) and the coaches. The newspapers are going to say what they want. People in Tampa, Orlando, Miami, they're going to write what they want to write."

Despite a tough loss at Auburn and some not-so-convincing wins in the second half of the season, Florida went back to the SEC Championship Game for the first time since 2000.

There, the Gators rolled to an early 17-0 lead before falling behind 21-17 against Arkansas, thanks in part to a pair of Leak interceptions in the third quarter.

But Leak led the Gators to their third straight come-from-behind win 38-28. He finally had that championship that he had worked so hard to get.

The first start of Chris Leak's career came one week after the Gators lost at home to Tennessee. *The Gainesville Sun*

On the same day, Southern Cal lost to UCLA. It was up to the voters who would play for the national championship. Florida jumped over Michigan into second in the BCS and would play Ohio State for the title in Glendale, Arizona.

THE GAME OF MY LIFE
BY CHRIS LEAK

It's funny because before that Arkansas game, I told Verne Lundquist of CBS, "One more to go." I wasn't thinking about another game. That SEC Championship Game was everything to me. Everything after that was a bonus to me. I played that game like it was my last game of the season.

What people don't know was that I strained my throwing thumb in the second quarter and had to get a shot at halftime. The whole third quarter, my hand was numb. But we were able to get the victory and the SEC championship.

The next day, we had seen that the coaches' poll moved us up to second so I had a feeling we were going to Glendale. And then when they called all of us and told us to meet in the stadium's press lounge to watch the announcement, I figured that was it.

Coach Meyer put this big board up where we ate every day and it was covered with all of these stories about how we were supposed to lose. I think for the older guys, like Dallas Baker and myself, we motivate ourselves. That was more for the younger guys, the 2006 class, to let them know how serious the game was. We already understood how serious it was.

We had a month to watch them on tape, and we saw that they played a bend-don't-break defense. A lot of zone coverage. You play a team like Arkansas and it's all man-to-man, it's hard to complete a lot of passes. Guys might get jammed on the line of scrimmage.

Ohio State had forced a turnover in every game so my main focus was not to turn the ball over. No turnovers, manage the game, spread the ball around. Those were my main thoughts.

I figured their offense would score a lot of points. As a quarterback, I had to anticipate a high-scoring game. And then Ted Ginn Jr. ran the opening kickoff back for a touchdown and it was just like I thought—a shoot-out.

That's why that first drive was so important. I knew we had to take advantage of every possession.

Watching them on tape, they never blitzed the first two series of a game. But against us, they blitzed every play in the first two series. But we had a lot of quick passes ready and I was able to check into the right protections. You see a team for a month and you can recognize things like that.

It was important to get into a good rhythm with my receivers and I did. I completed my first five passes on that drive. On the touchdown to Dallas, we had four receivers to one side and he was alone on the other. Usually, you run a slant from that formation and the cornerback tried to jump the route. But I pumped for the slant and Dallas adjusted, and I tossed it over the cornerback's head for the touchdown.

We got the ball back and went right down and scored again. And then we scored again. They were dropping eight and when you spread a team like that out it wears down the linebackers. We were throwing five-yard passes and their linebackers were 15 yards deep.

People have asked me how it felt to complete all of those passes. It just felt normal to me. I had that game where I completed 17 in a row.

I hit a big pass to Cornelius Ingram that helped us get another score. That was my best throw of the game. I think it affected their safeties the rest of the game.

At halftime, we were ahead 34-14, but I kept telling myself it was zero-zero. Coach always says the game doesn't have to be close. We can make it close but it doesn't have to be. The way we were moving the ball and the way our defense was playing, it wasn't close, but you have to have the mentality that it still is.

The first play of the half, the snap was high and went over my head. I probably should have caught it. I found it and threw it out of bounds, so that was a big play, just avoiding the turnover.

That was the best thing about the whole deal from the opening kickoff to that play to everything. It was straight composure, straight calm in the huddle. Nobody ever got frustrated.

In the fourth quarter, I had a 14-yard run on a quarterback draw to set up our last touchdown. You play a team that zones, you have to hit some quarterback draws. That kills the defense. The linebackers have no idea where the ball is going.

The last snap, I took a knee and threw the ball in the air. You can't explain the feeling. The only thing I can say is it's overwhelming. At the same time, for me and the older guys, all the stuff we had been through, the summer workouts, the two-a-days, all the hard work, it was like a big weight off my shoulders.

I remember watching Vince Young after Texas won it the year before. there was a shot of him with the trophy and the confetti, a shot from behind him. I saw that and I wanted it to happen to me.

THE AFTERMATH

Leak was named the Most Valuable Player for the BCS National Championship Game and the Gators were welcomed home at halftime of the next day's basketball game to a prolonged standing ovation.

Four days later, 70,000 people showed up in The Swamp for a celebration. Former UF quarterback Danny Wuerffel, the only other Florida quarterback to win a national championship, presented Leak with the MVP trophy.

Chapter 19

WILBER MARSHALL

PREGAME

Marshall grew up as one of 11 children in Mims, Florida., on the outskirts of Titusville, Florida. There he had to avoid more than blockers. Mims was a rough town with its share of violence.

But Marshall stayed clear of problems by playing sports, working the citrus groves with members of his family and listening to his parents. He was too big to play youth football and had to wait until he went to Titusville Astronaut High to show what he could do.

The story goes that when Marshall was a junior varsity player, he took a ball in each hand and dunked them both in one leap. The Astronaut coach immediately promoted him to the varsity.

Marshall was an excellent basketball player and a track star as well, but it was in football where he really excelled. He never left the field, having waterboys bring shoes for different duties, whether it be offense, defense, or special teams.

Heavily recruited, he considered Florida State and Ohio State before deciding on the new coach at Florida—Charley Pell—who promised Marshall a chance to play his favorite position, tight end.

"My high school coach, Jay Donnelly, went to Florida," Marshall said. "Being from Florida, this was the place to be. All of my friends were at Florida. And it was a new start. We had a chance to build Florida football from the ground up.

"Players who were part of that recruiting class would call me and tell me, 'We can win with you.' (Running back) James Jones, who came in the year before, called and said, 'This is the place to be.' But really, Coach Pell talked me into it."

Pell's first year was a struggle to say the least. Florida went 0-10-1, tying Georgia Tech and losing the rest of the games that season. UF had ousted Doug Dickey following a tumultuous 1978 season, and Pell came to Florida with plenty of promise.

But first, he had to get things cleaned up. Before his death from cancer at 60, Pell told me that his first season at Florida "was the year I was introduced to the DEA. We had one player who called me the night before a game because his roommate was smoking pot. I sent someone to his room to take it and the following Monday the player came in demanding his pot. Can you believe that?"

It was an uneasy situation for a kid from Mims, but Pell had put together an excellent recruiting class that featured quarterback Wayne Peace. In 1980, Florida put together the biggest turnaround at the time in the history of college football, going 8-4 and winning the Tangerine Bowl.

Marshall played sparingly at tight end that season, mostly playing special teams. Florida was loaded at tight end with Chris Faulkner and Mike Mularkey.

But he remembers his introduction to Florida Field.

"Running through that tunnel, for a guy from a small town, it was scary," he said. "It was definitely something different. But I fed off the fans. They stayed with us. You felt like you could walk on water out there."

During the spring of 1981, Pell asked Marshall to move to linebacker where the Gators were still thin.

Marshall was so devastated he almost quit, but stayed at the urging of his parents. Pell eventually acquiesed, telling Marshall he'd leave him at tight end but the team really needed him at outside linebacker.

Marshall decided to go ahead and make the switch, a move that would change his life forever. Nobody will ever know just how good he could have been on offense, but there was no question how good he was on the defensive side of the ball.

As a sophomore, Marshall led the team with 121 tackles and what was then a school-record 11 sacks.

Even bigger things were expected of his junior season. By then his bond with Pell had grown strong. Marshall often served as a baby-sitter for the Pell's son, Carrick, and the two formed a tight friendship.

As the 1982 season rolled around, everything was lined up for a big year from the tight end-turned-linebacker.

The Gators opened the season with a huge win against Miami in Gainesville and it was huge day for Marshall as well.

The winning score came when Peace rolled to his right and lofted a pass for Jones who made a one-handed grab at the goal line, falling into the end zone. It is known in Gator lore as simply "The Catch."

Marshall had 17 tackles that day against the Hurricanes, racing all over the field to corral Miami running backs and pressure quarterback Jim Kelly. The 17-14 victory was important for Florida, but the Gators knew that the real challenge would come the following week.

Once the hoopla and celebrations ended for the spectacular win over arch-rival Miami, Florida found out it was on the edge of the Associated Press Top 10 at No. 11. One spot ahead? The Trojans, coached by legendary John Robinson.

It would be USC's first and only visit to Gainesville, which had fans and media buzzing. More than anything, this would be Florida's opportunity to show it was a legitimate college football power.

One thing favoring the Gators was the artificial turf and humidity that came with playing at Florida Field. USC brought plenty of tradition while Florida fans were still only a year removed from 0-10-1.

THE GAME OF MY LIFE
BY WILBER MARSHALL

Everybody on our team was so close then. We lived in Yon Hall and we considered it a fraternity, all the athletes. We used to call it "Yon Phi Yon." All of the athletes pulled for each other in whatever sport we were playing.

The week before we were to play Southern Cal, we knew it was a huge game. We felt like this was the game to put us on the map. We were

Despite knee and hip problems, Wilber Marshall loves to play golf and does so whenever he can. *University of Florida archives*

up and coming, but this was the game that would be a big deal nationally if we could win. They were coming from all the way across the country and they had all the tradition. We wanted to show the world that this is where real football is played.

It was so hot that day. We played on astroturf then and you could rub your hands across it and get burned. We had these dugouts where we'd sit with big ice blocks to cool us down. And we had Gatorade. I think we were the guinea pigs for frozen Gatorade. They'd freeze it and put it in these cups and we'd eat them one after the other. It really helped.

I remember in the locker room it was real quiet before the game. It was the old locker room where the visiting teams dress now, not like the new locker room they have now. But it was real quiet because we knew what was on the line. Everyone knew they were coming to our house and we wanted to show them the kind of defense the Gators played.

They had their one play—student body right or student body left—where they would leave the outside linebacker on the side away from where the play was going unblocked because he wasn't supposed to be able to chase the back and get to him before he turned the corner. But I kept chasing him down every time.

He'd wait for his blocks, kind of hesitate as he got to the spot where he was supposed to turn up, and I'd just sprint to him and tackle him. They'd run it to the strong side a lot in that game and I'd be on the weak side and just run down the line to the running back. I had a bunch of tackles (14) and most of them came on that student body play. They kept running it over and over and letting me run through the backfield. It was a lot of fun.

I felt like I was unblockable. They'd throw on third down and I'd just rush the passer. They'd try to block me with a back and I'd just go right by him or through him and get to the quarterback. Their quarterback was Sean Salisbury. He's on television now. That's where he belongs. He wasn't very good.

We didn't do much on offense but we didn't have to because our defense was so good and they couldn't block me or didn't block me. We were ahead 17-9 and I got to Salisbury on their last drive to put it away.

It was a challenge for me because I was going against the big guys. They had Bruce Matthews on the offensive line and some other guys who went on to the NFL, but they couldn't do anything against us.

I think it was one of my best games ever. I just kept running around the corner, tackling guys or disrupting the play. It was a great feeling, even thought it was so hot, to be out there and just blowing up so many plays.

The crowd was going wild, and after the game they stayed in the stands. They didn't want to leave. Coach Pell went back out there and led the team in a victory lap around the stadium.

But I didn't go back out there. I was beat. It was so hot and I'd been running around so much, I was finished. Just beat. I had left everything I had on the field. Everything. I had nothing left. I didn't want to go back out there on that hot astroturf.

But it was an important game for us and for the University of Florida. Everything has grown so much in Gainesville, the buildings, the stadium was nowhere near as big as it is now. Where there used to be fields, there are buildings. The facilities are amazing. I'd like to think I had a piece of it.

THE AFTERMATH

While Gainesville celebrated into the night following the win over USC, the season hit a ditch later with consecutive losses to LSU and Vanderbilt. The Gators were ranked fourth in the nation when they were beaten at home by the Tigers 24-13 and followed that up with a two-point loss in Nashville.

Then came Jacksonville.

After consecutive down-to-the-wire losses to Georgia in 1980 and 1981, the Gators failed to show up for the 1982 game in the Gator Bowl. Nothing went right for UF, everything went right for the Bulldogs, who won 44-0.

The Gators rebounded to win three straight before falling to Arkansas in the Bluebonnet Bowl and entered Marshall's senior season unranked. Florida demolished Miami in the Orange Bowl 28-3 to open the season, then suffered an improbable tie in the return trip to Southern Cal. In that game, Florida was penalized on what should have been the final play of a 19-13 win, giving USC one more chance. The Trojans scored, then missed the extra point.

Florida won five straight before suffering back-to-back losses at Auburn and to Georgia in Jacksonville. In the final home game of Marshall's career at UF, the Gators hammered FSU 53-14, and as he was being interviewed by ABC, Marshall was overwhelmed by fans chanting his name. He jumped on the dugout and began slapping hands with appreciative Gator fans.

Marshall was the 11th pick of the ensuing NFL Draft by Chicago and played a major part in the 1985 Bears winning the world championship. He also won a Super Bowl playing for Washington in 1992. In 12 seasons with five teams, Marshall had 45 sacks and 23 interceptions, three of which he returned for touchdowns. He played 179 games in his NFL career.

Marshall splits time between his two homes. The rigors of the NFL have taken their toll on Marshall, a pair of knees crying to be replaced and a bad back, but he managed his money well enough to still enjoy his life.

Chapter 20

SHANE MATTHEWS

OKLAHOMA STATE AT FLORIDA
SEPTEMBER 8, 1990
FLORIDA FIELD

PREGAME

Shane Matthews started throwing a football around as soon as he was old enough to walk. The son of the head football coach at Cleveland High in Mississippi, Matthews was always hanging around practice, kicking footballs and throwing them to imaginary targets.

The skinny kid stepped into the quarterback job in seventh grade and kept the job through junior high school.

"Throwing a football just came naturally to me," he said. "But the sport I really liked the best was baseball. I played basketball, too, and I liked both of those sports better than football because the practices were more fun. Football practice in Mississippi is really hot."

Despite the fact that his father was the head football coach, he never pressured his son into sports. When they left the football facilities every day, they never talked about football. It was something to be left on the practice field.

But there did come a point when the family had plenty to talk about. Matthews' father was offered the head coaching job at Pascagoula High in the southern part of the state. By then, Shane had so many friends, so many teammates, that his mother and father decided the decision would be left up to their son as he prepared to enter the 10th grade.

"We went down there and looked at everything," Matthews said. "It was going to be hard for me to leave. But the facility down there was awesome. They seated 15,000 people in their stadium. The locker room was 100 yards long. The baseball field was unbelievable.

"It was like taking a step up. I knew this could help me get to the next level. But it wasn't easy. I had grown up with those guys in Cleveland and I was their quarterback and now I'm leaving?"

The decision was made to move to Pascagoula where Shane's dad would be the head coach and Shane the starting quarterback. After a pair of 7-3 seasons, Matthews guided the team to a 15-0 record and a state championship as a senior.

"We were loaded," he said. "We had 98 players on our team. We had Terrell Buckley and Kez McCorvey, who both ended up at FSU. We had three guys sign with LSU and a few more go to Mississippi State. We just blew everybody out.

"But it was hard playing for your dad. The people in the community will always say the only reason you're playing is because your dad is the coach. But I knew my dad was only going to play the best players. He was hard on me, but I think that prepared me to play at the next level and to play for Steve Spurrier."

Texas A&M had been recruiting Matthews since before his junior season because Jackie Sherrill, who was then the coach, grew up in Buloxi and was familiar with Mississippi high school football. Some schools, like Alabama, backed off the lanky quarterback because they figured his fate was sealed.

"My dad played at Ole Miss and my mom was a cheerleader at Ole Miss," Matthews said. "A lot of people figured it was a no-brainer. But I wanted to play big-time football. I went to some Ole Miss games and it didn't seem like big-time football."

Matthews took his four visits to A&M, FSU, LSU, and Florida. After each visit, the family would sit down with a sheet of paper and list the pros and cons of each school. Matthews decided early that Texas A&M wasn't going to happen. His best friend, center Frankie Godfrey, had signed with LSU, only 3½ hours from home. It was tempting.

His mother liked Florida's academics and didn't feel right about FSU. Matthews couldn't have cared less about academics, but he did like the atmosphere at Florida, and it offered a chance to get away.

"I always said if I had gone to Florida State, they'd have never known who Charlie Ward was," Matthews said. "He and I were the two quarterbacks they were recruiting."

Ward, of course, won the Heisman Trophy in 1993. By then, Matthews had started his professional career. But it wasn't an easy journey from Florida signee to starting quarterback.

In his first season, Matthews was redshirted. At 165 pounds, he needed to add some weight to his frame to be ready for the SEC.

"I was extremely skinny and I just couldn't put weight on," he said. "By the time I finished at Florida, I was up to 180 and got up to 200 in the NFL."

The following year, Matthews was buried on the depth chart while Kyle Morris started at quarterback. After an opening loss to Ole Miss, the Gators started to get things going before a season turned ugly.

An NCAA investigation, the firing of Galen Hall as head coach after five games, and then a gambling scandal that forced the school to suspend Morris for the rest of the season.

When the names of the other players involved were announced, hardly anyone blinked at the name Shane Matthews.

"It was a learning experience for all of us," Matthews said. "It wasn't a big deal, just a few of us betting on some games with some frat boys. I was just trying to pay for all the parking tickets I had. But when I look back, it was good for me. My dad had always told me that once you started something you finished it. I was ready to leave and go to Ole Miss. All my buddies who didn't get scholarships were there and they told me I could play right away. But my dad told me that I was staying for the duration. He just said, 'Nope. You're going to graduate from Florida.'"

With the program in turmoil, Florida turned to its favorite son—Steve Spurrier—to be the next coach.

"I didn't know him at all," Matthews said. "My dad and I watched Duke's bowl game and we both thought the offense was right up my alley."

Florida's spring game in 1990 was played in Jacksonville while construction took place at Florida Field on an expanded north end zone.

In 1992 with two true freshmen starting at tackles, Shane Matthews willed the Gators into the SEC Championship Game. *The Gainesville Sun*

"I remember my dad, who never would say anything about his son not playing, telling Coach Spurrier one day at practice that if he gave me a chance, I could run the offense," Matthews said. "And (quarterbacks coach) John Reaves was a big fan of mine. He was coaching the Orange and he picked me to be his quarterback."

Matthews threw three touchdowns that day while Morris, playing for the Blue team, threw four interceptions. While Spurrier didn't make it official after the spring game, it was obvious he was leaning toward Matthews to start the first game of the Spurrier Era at Florida.

The opponent would be Oklahoma State, a team dealing with NCAA problems of its own. Sanctions had damaged the Cowboys' program. It wouldn't get any better during their trip to Gainesville.

THE GAME OF MY LIFE
BY SHANE MATTHEWS

Coach Spurrier let us know about a week before the game that I was going to be the starter. I kind of had a feeling it was going to happen. But I didn't know if he was going to have the guts to name this guy nobody had ever heard of to start the first game he ever coached at his alma mater.

Kyle wasn't happy, but he never resented me. He and I were and still are very close. He was disappointed but he was happy for me.

I was ecstatic. I kept it inside because I keep things inside, but I couldn't wait to call my dad and tell him. Any time you're getting ready to start your first game at quarterback at one of the Big Three schools in the state, you know the media attention will be overwhelming and it was. But Coach Spurrier was always good about keeping the media away from his players unless it was required.

I don't get real excited, but I was before that game. It was the first game of the Spurrier Era, the fans didn't know what to expect. No matter what level you're at, if you don't get butterflies before a game, that's when you need to get out. If you don't feel that rush of adrenaline, you need to stop playing. Well, I was feeling it.

The night before in the hotel, there was so much running through my head. What if they do this? What if they run this coverage? What do you check to? I didn't know what to expect. I'd never thrown a pass in a college football game.

I listened to my CD player on the way to the game, some country and some Guns 'n' Roses. Driving down North-South Drive, that's when the chill bumps get you. I remember pulling on my jersey thinking, "Oh, boy. This is big-time college football. This is why you play."

There was a lot of pressure, but once we got out there and warmed up, I calmed down. Coach Spurrier asked me in the pregame what I wanted to call for my first play. I wanted a draw or a screen. A quarterback always likes a screen to get that first completion. But he said, "Shoot, we're going to throw it down the field." And I was thinking, "Oh, Lord."

The first play was Trips Left Zip Blue Slide Z Red Cross. I hit Ernie Mills for about 25 yards. He was wide open. Then we ran a couple and we ran a steamers route and I hit Ernie again for about 25 yards. Dexter

McNabb, our fullback, scored on the next play. It took us five plays and I was thinking this was so easy.

Coach was fired up, too. He had confidence in us but he wasn't sure how I'd handle things. The rest of the game was pretty much the same thing. He had us so prepared and everything we prepared for was happening on the field. I hit Tre Everett on a deep post for a touchdown. We were kind of relieved to be up by so much at the half, but Coach wanted to put up as many points as possible. That was his philosophy. We ended up scoring 50 and won 50-7. I didn't play the whole game because we were ahead by so much.

After the game, there were reporters everywhere and cameras. I was on Cloud Nine. But Coach Spurrier told us it wouldn't be as easy the next week at Alabama. He made sure we understood. Still, it was great for our confidence to see where we were at and it was great for me to get off to such a good start. I missed some throws and there was room to improve, but it was a day I'll never forget.

THE AFTERMATH

Florida won at Alabama the following week, but midway through the season the Gators received the bad news that they would be ineligible for the SEC title because of infractions committed by the previous coaching staff.

"We painted our shoes black the rest of the year," Matthews said. "Nobody on that team was involved in any of the infractions. We didn't think it was right."

Florida finished first in the SEC and the players received rings saying as much. To this day, Spurrier pushes to have that team recognized as SEC champions. The following year, Matthews and the Gators got one for real.

Florida went unbeaten in SEC play in 1991 to claim the school's first official title. The celebrations spilled onto University Ave.

The following year, Matthews somehow got Florida to the first SEC Championship Game, where the Gators lost to Alabama 28-21 when a Matthews pass was intercepted and returned for a touchdown.

"Unfortunately," he said, "that's the game I remember the most."

Matthews went on to the NFL where he played with several teams, including Washington for Spurrier again.

During a time-out in a game late in his sophomore year, Matthews was taken aback by a Florida cheerleader on the sidelines.

"I've got to get to know her," he thought to himself.

He eventually married Stephanie Weldon and the couple have two children, Brooke and Luke, and are settled in Gainesville now that Matthews has retired from football. He has an interest in coaching, but only if he can stay in Gainesville.

Chapter 21

LEE
McGRIFF

PREGAME

McGriff was born in Gainesville where his dad was the captain of the UF track team and started the sports program at P.K. Yonge. But when he was nine years old, his parents split and McGriff moved to Tampa with his mother.

He not only had to leave his friends behind, but his beloved Gators.

"I was (former UF quarterback) Larry Libertore," he said. "That was the first guy I was a big fan of. I was a bat boy for the baseball team. So I wasn't just leaving my dad and my friends, but everything that had to do with athletics. My world was turned upside down."

The transition didn't turn out to be so difficult, because when he arrived in Tampa he found himself surrounded by Florida fans. He was befriended by future Gator football player Jimbo Kynes and future UF baseball player Bubba Huerta.

He spent his days at the Anderson playground in Tampa, playing every sport possible until the sun went down. In eighth grade, he made the junior high team at Wilson. The next year he was to be the starting wingback, but the county put a weight restriction in place that year.

"You had to be 115 pounds and I was 105," he said. "I can say it now that it broke my heart. All of my friends were playing and I was the guy on the sidelines watching."

A growth spurt allowed McGriff to try out for the junior varsity team at Plant High the next year where he played well enough to be elevated to the varsity at the end of the season.

After a solid junior season, he led the Western Conference in receiving as a senior and still didn't make the all-conference first team. But he was not getting the attention of college recruiters.

"It's not like the colleges were saying, 'There's this kid McGriff in Tampa. Let's go sign him.' Nobody recruited me," he said.

One coach from Richmond did stop by Plant to look at McGriff, said he was considering signing the diminutive wide receiver, then never called back.

McGriff had hoped to sign with Florida. After attending camp in Gainesville, then-coach Ray Graves told him they would "find a place for me at Florida." But by the time he was finished at Plant, Doug Dickey had taken over as the coach at UF.

McGriff's father called Florida wide receiver coach Bubba McGowan and Graves trying to get Florida to take a look. There was some interest from Auburn, but the Tigers used their final scholarship on a lineman. Miami defensive coordinator Charlie Bailey made a visit, worked McGriff out and told him he was too small.

Dickey had visited the McGriff home during the Christmas holidays because he had played for McGriff's father at P.K. Yonge.

"He told me, 'You are not ready to play at the University of Florida. Maybe you should try junior college,'" McGriff said. "I thought my dad was going to kill him right there on the spot. At that point, I wanted to play for someone who was going to play against Florida."

McGriff attended the Orange and Blue game in the spring of 1971, meeting with Graves (then the athletic director) in an empty stadium after the game was over. Graves told him he belonged at UF and that he should walk on to the team.

"I knew I could play," he said. "I'd work there for the maintenance department in the summers and work out with the team, catching balls from John Reaves. I knew I could do what they were doing."

So he decided to give Florida a try. The Gators had signed a pair of *Parade* All-Americans and were loaded at wide receiver.

"But from the first day I knew I was better than they were," he said.

He started for the freshman team and had one game against Miami where he caught 10 passes, three for touchdowns. After the game, Dickey found McGriff in the shower and told him he'd be on scholarship the following year.

As a sophomore, McGriff alternated with the other wide receivers, usually just to bring in plays. But before a game against Auburn, Dickey told McGriff the Gators were going to try something different. McGriff was on the field for only 10 plays.

"The next week in practice, we're out in shorts and I'm doing everything at full speed," he said. "I got in fights all day. Coach Dickey came out of his tower and pulled me off the field. I told him, 'I will break everybody's legs if you sit me down again.' I kept that going for the rest of my life."

McGriff started the next week and never let go of the job.

Like so many other years, 1973 was supposed to be the Year of the Gator. Florida had a sensational tailback named Nat Moore and a veteran team led by quarterback David Bowden.

But in a 33-12 loss to Mississippi State in Jackson, Mississippi, Moore suffered a knee injury that would keep him out for most of the rest of the season.

It was a season that went down quickly.

Losses to LSU and Alabama by a combined score of 59-17 followed. Against Ole Miss the following week, Bowden threw a fourth-down pass out of bounds to stop the clock, not realizing Florida had failed to pick up a first down on the previous play, and the Gators lost 13-10.

The Year of the Gator was in ruins. With an open date the following week, Dickey decided to make a change at quarterback. He inserted the more mobile Don Gaffney into the starting line-up.

"David Bowden was one of my favorite people in the world," McGriff said. "It broke my heart."

Florida had never won at Auburn, but pulled out an improbable 12-8 victory with Gaffney at the controls and Vince Kendrick playing a stellar game at tailback. Florida was still only 3-4 on the season, but there was hope heading into the annual game against Georgia in Jacksonville.

THE GAME OF MY LIFE
BY LEE McGRIFF

Back then, and it was also when Steve Spurrier was the coach because we used to talk about it, playing Auburn and Georgia back-to-back was a real issue. We'd leave everything on the field against Auburn and have a hard time with Georgia. Georgia would play us and then Auburn, and they'd always struggle with Auburn.

The Auburn game was such an emotional win, but we weren't going to have a letdown. After that game, we wanted to get back out on the field and play again.

The night before the game, we went to the movies and just as our bus pulled up, so did another one carrying the Georgia team. We were going to the same movie. Coach Dickey got out of our bus and Vince Dooley out of theirs and they started talking. You could have cut the tension with a knife. Who was going to back down? We ended up both going to the same movie.

We got to the game and there was a cold wind blowing, really hard so we knew we weren't going to throw it much. Coach Dickey was a conservative guy anyway. We couldn't get anything going offensively. He called some screens, some options, really close to the vest.

It seemed like the score was 7-3 all day long. But that's the way a lot of football games were played in those days, low scoring.

They kicked a field goal late to make it 10-3 and the clock was winding down and we knew if we were going to win it, we had to do it now. We had 80 yards to go into the wind.

The first drive, we got to third down and I ran a quick post. Don gunned it and it went over my head, but the Georgia defender hit me from behind as I was getting ready to jump. I don't know if I would have made the first down. It would have been close.

We ran it a couple of times, another third down, and I ran a streak up the right sideline. The wind made the ball wobble and I just laid out and caught it. I was ready to do whatever I had to do to make the play.

Lee McGriff was first-team All-SEC in 1974 despite Florida going to the wishbone offense that season. *University of Florida archives*

We got another big third-down conversion to Joel Parker. It seemed like we converted a lot of third downs on that drive.

We got to the 20 and had another third down and they called a screen. It was a great call. It was set up perfectly. Don threw it to Vince Kendrick, who had great hands. He threw it perfectly. And Vince dropped it. Vince was an unbelievable player who was the guy you wanted to throw the ball to in that situation. But he dropped it.

So it was fourth down and we had to go for it. I was supposed to run a curl but I knew I had to run it a little deeper to get into the end zone. I got into the end zone and turned and came charging back, trying to find a hole.

Don let it rip. He was one second away from getting killed, but Burton Lawless made a block for him.

I saw the ball coming high and I had to get it. That's all. I gave it all I had. It was high and hot. I didn't think, I just had to get it. And I did for the touchdown. Then, I did something I've never done in my life. I threw it straight up in the air. Jimmy Ray Stephens caught it and handed it to the official, but he still threw the flag, so we were going to have a 15-yard penalty on the kickoff.

We were going to go for two to try to win it. We really had no choice. I wanted the ball again. I was on fire.

I was open, but Don went to our tight end Hank Foldberg. He caught it for the two-point conversion to put us up 11-10.

They got the ball back and they couldn't do much with it. They did what they had been doing the whole game, and we stopped them.

I was coaching during the Lindsay Scott game when he went 93 yards for the winning score in 1980. I promise you, those guys in 1973 didn't feel one thing we didn't feel that day.

The ground was shaking. It was dizzying. It was wild in the locker room. Just delirious.

THE AFTERMATH

With Gaffney at quarterback, Florida salvaged its season with what was known then as "A November to Remember." In addition to Auburn and Georgia, the Gators closed with wins over Kentucky, Miami, and Florida State, beating the Seminoles 49-0.

The Tangerine Bowl wanted the Gators, but Florida used its muscle to insists that the game be played in Gainesville. On a bitter cold night, Miami of Ohio (with a defensive back named Ron Zook) prevailed 16-7, putting a damper on a special season.

With the Gaffney-to-McGriff hook-up working 36 times the following season, Florida went 8-3, losing this time to Georgia when a late two-point conversion failed this time. The Gators went to the Sugar Bowl where they couldn't hold a 10-0 lead and lost to Nebraska 13-10.

McGriff signed a free agent contract with Dallas but was cut the week of the first game. The Cowboys went on to win the Super Bowl.

He joined the World Football league and played in Dallas for three games before being traded to Charlotte. That league folded and McGriff ended up with the Tampa Bay Bucs for their inaugural season. After being cut in November, McGriff knew his family was about to begin with the arrival of a son and rather than go play in Canada or go to an NFL camp, he decided to try coaching.

"I knew I needed a more stable job," he said.

His first stint was under Bobby Bowden at Florida State, but Gainesville called him back when Doug Dickey hired him. McGriff stayed through the coaching transition to Charley Pell, but in 1983 decided he'd had enough of the coaching profession.

"It was a hard decision to get out of coaching," he said.

He settled in Gainesville with his family and began selling insurance.

McGriff served as the color analyst for Florida games on the radio but left the booth when his son Travis began playing for the Gators. Three years ago, he decided to get back into radio and works the Gator games with Mick Hubert while still running a thriving insurance business in Gainesville.

Chapter 22

TRAVIS McGRIFF

PREGAME

Travis McGriff was born in Tampa, Florida, where his father, Lee, was in training camp with the Tampa Bay Bucs. At the age of two, he moved to Gainesville when his father became the wide receivers coach at UF.

At an early age he realized that his father wasn't only a coach, but had been one of Florida's all-time great receivers.

"Pretty quickly I knew about football and the Gators," he said. "By the time I was three or four, I had a pretty strong sense that he was a player and a pretty good one."

McGriff stepped right into the athletic scene as a youngster playing football and basketball at the Boys' Club and basketball in the city league. Despite his small size, he was effective because of his speed and discipline.

But the position he played in football until he got to college wasn't receiver but quarterback. He went to Buchholz High and played as a back-up to Dale Scott on a state championship team as a freshman and was the starter as a sophomore.

167

But at Buchholz, there weren't a lot of opportunities for a quarterback to show off his skills. The Bobcats were an effective running team with future Gator Tyrone Baker carrying the load.

"All we did was run it," McGriff said. "Nobody went both ways. Tyrone Baker was our running back and we had a wonderful offensive line. We just ran it down people's throats. Why throw it?

"I was starting to worry and Dad was starting to wonder. If I was going to play college football it was not going to be as a quarterback when I was getting a chance to run around and throw it."

McGriff transferred before his junior season to P.K. Yonge where former Gator John Clifford was the coach. The Blue Wave was loaded with talent at the skill positions with future NFL players like Terry Jackson and Robert Baker.

"It was the best decision we could have made," McGriff said. "John Clifford was loose, liked to throw the ball around. We were really good. It was a good move.

"I played quarterback and corner, and every once in a while if we wanted to go deep they'd stick me out there. I loved it. It was fun and I loved the chance to play defense."

McGriff had already received a recruiting letter from Notre Dame as a sophomore and after his junior year, when P.K. Yonge lost in the semifinals of the state playoffs, the recruiting interest intensified.

Plenty of schools wanted McGriff but at different positions.

Kentucky was still running the option and wanted him to play quarterback. Arkansas recruited McGriff as a safety. Georgia Tech and Clemson were looking at him as a wide receiver. Florida and Florida State thought he could play either defensive back or wide receiver.

Before his senior year, McGriff went to a summer football camp at Notre Dame.

"I just wanted to see it," he said. "It was beautiful, a lot of history and tradition. But I knew that I couldn't go there. It was way up north and cold and I couldn't identify with the teams they were playing. It wasn't me.

"So it was Florida or Florida State. Looking back, I was an idiot. I should have used all my visits and enjoyed myself. But it was during basketball season, and I didn't want to miss any games."

Besides, his mind had been made up on a late November day in 1993.

Travis McGriff has been involved in both the Arena Football League and the new All-American Football League. *The Gainesville Sun*

McGriff went to the Florida-FSU game in Gainesville and decided he would walk into the stadium totally neutral to see how it felt.

"I really thought I might go to FSU," he said. "They were spreading the ball around and it was a great program, a great situation. The FSU coaches made you feel like the program was going to fall apart if you didn't come. Steve Spurrier, you know how he is. 'Got a scholarship, Trav. Want it?'

"So I decided to go to this game and be neutral. I could not do it. I was pulling for Florida with everything I had. In the final hour, the allegiances were too powerful for me to go anywhere but Florida."

He played in UF's first three games as a true freshman, catching a few passes but falling a bit behind Reidel Anthony and Ike Hilliard. In line at the training table the following week, he learned about the medical redshirt.

"Spurrier came up to me and said, 'Trav, my man, is that hamstring bothering you?' I told him it was fine. But he said, 'No, I think it's bothering you. You better go see (trainer) Chris Patrick.' It took me a minute but I caught on that they wanted me to medical redshirt. So I ended up redshirting, which was a good thing."

The following season, injuries to two Florida cornerbacks meant McGriff would switch over to defense. He loved playing it in high school, but that was when he was also playing offense.

"If I'm not going to play offense anymore, I don't know if loved it anymore," he said.

But he was moved back to offense and contributed on back-to-back teams that played for national titles, winning it in 1996. But McGriff missed the second half of that championship season with a torn ACL.

In '97, Anthony and Hilliard had left early for the NFL and it would be Jacquez Green and McGriff as the primary targets. Mostly, it was Green.

"Coach Spurrier worked really hard to feed the ball to Quez," McGriff said. "As much as I wanted to believe I was healthy, I wasn't right. Quez was getting fed the ball and I think it hurt the offense. Nobody had really been fed like that before."

Green left for the NFL the following spring and Florida turned to McGriff as the No. 1 receiver.

While McGriff was having a record-breaking year, Florida found itself in an unusual position. For the first time since 1992, the Gators lost to Tennessee in Knoxville when Florida had seven turnovers and still took the game to overtime.

The Vols would go on to win the national championship, but as the season progressed, Florida was still in the running for both the league and national titles.

Six straight wins over SEC opponents, including a 38-7 beating of Georgia in Jacksonville, had returned UF to the top five in the national polls.

To close out the SEC season, the Gators would face South Carolina on Homecoming. It was also Senior Day, the last home game for the Florida seniors who still had hopes that this could be a special year.

It was a special game for one of Florida's seniors.

THE GAME OF MY LIFE
BY TRAVIS McGRIFF

That 1998 team was a great team, different than the '96 team, but a great team. We had an incredible defense, and Doug Johnson and Jesse Palmer had a lot of trust in me. But I wasn't getting fed the ball. It just worked out because of the relationships I had with the quarterbacks.

Senior Day wasn't overly emotional for me because I had so much else to think about. We were still in the top five in the country. I knew it was my last game in The Swamp, but when you're about to play a game, you notice the outside circumstances, but I was thinking about the way South Carolina was going to cover me.

I was in the tunnel, waiting to be introduced, but I was thinking about the game. When you're in there, guys are in front of you and you don't really see the crowd or the parents on the field. Then you go out and it is kind of a rush of emotion. Seeing my parents, it was kind of emotional, but as soon as it's over, that's gone and you have a game to play.

We liked the way we matched up with them. They played a lot of zone and when they went to man defense we didn't think they could match up with our receivers. So the plan was to throw it around a bunch and beat them to death, which was always the game plan.

And we did. Travis Taylor had over 100 yards receiving and I had a big day—13 catches for 222 yards.

The thing I really remember was very early I knew it was going to be a big day. Everything I did was working. Routes that weren't supposed to be coming to me were coming to me. It felt like I had a slew of catches really early and we were beating them easily. I remember thinking this might really be a big game for me.

Midway through the second quarter, I caught my first touchdown on a post pattern. Their defender kind of rolled my ankle as I was scoring. My ankle had been beaten up for weeks. It was really hurting. I thought I should come out because we had them beat and we had Florida State the next week and maybe the SEC Championship Game.

All of those things were going through my head. I couldn't ruin myself in that game because we had too much left.

But selfishly, I thought these balls are coming to me, and it's too easy, too much fun. There's no way I'm coming out of this game. They re-taped it, didn't shoot it up or anything, and I went back in.

When I really knew it was a good day was on the last touchdown. I was hobbling on a bad ankle and the defender was playing bump coverage on me so Doug checked to a fade. It was my right ankle that was my stiff leg if I were going to make a move and get past this guy to run a fade. I couldn't do it. I'm trying to figure out in my head how I was going to do it.

Doug got the snap and it so happened the defensive back steps with his inside foot so I could kind of give him a little something and use my upper body to push him by. I couldn't have scripted it any better.

That's when I thought it couldn't go any better. If he stepped the other way, I was dead. Doug threw a perfect pass and I got the touchdown.

Now every Friday before a game I'd go to lunch with Dad, talk about whatever. He had been a big fan of Carlos Alvarez. That was his guy. So he told me the story about Carlos' last game at home. He had been struggling with his knees and everything and couldn't get deep anymore. But he got deep one last time and scored a touchdown. And then, because of everything that had happened, he threw the ball in the stands.

So Dad mentioned if you scored late and thought you might not get back in, you might want to throw it in stands. After we talked about it, I kind of forgot about it. But I was getting the sense late in the third quarter that we might start pulling the starters because we were way up.

So when I scored, I chunked it up into the south end zone stands. It was a good throw. I came off to the sidelines and Spurrier was mad because there was a penalty. "Was Trav dancing. What'd he do?" I told him I had thrown the ball in the stands. He looked at me and said, "All right my man. I was probably going to tell you to do that anyway."

It was a great way to end my home career. Carlos had written me a handwritten letter during the season saying that he enjoyed watching me play through years and he never wanted anyone to break his records. But he hoped I did. That meant a lot to me coming from someone who I had been hearing about for so long.

THE AFTERMATH

Florida dropped its final game of the regular season a week later in Tallahassee, losing to FSU 23-12. FSU would play Tennessee for the national title. McGriff scored the first touchdown of the game, but missed opportunities cost the Gators.

"After that first touchdown, I thought we were going to kill them," McGriff said.

Florida finished its season beating Syracuse 31-10 in the Orange Bowl. McGriff was drafted in the third round by the Denver Broncos, but had only five catches in three season. He also spent a year with the Atlanta Falcons before moving on to the Orlando Predators of the Arena Football League where he was the rookie of the year in 2003.

McGriff's football career ended after two-plus seasons of Arena Football, but he worked as the football stunt double for Mark Wahlberg in the movie *Invincible*.

McGriff has settled in Gainesville where he has several business ventures. He also has started a wide receivers camp.

"Just teaching that position," he said. "That position is so under-taught."

Chapter 23

NAT MOORE

PREGAME

Nat Moore covered the three big football powers in the state of Florida—he was born in Tallahassee, moved to Miami when he was five, and attended the University of Florida in Gainesville.

It was a difficult upbringing living in the projects in Miami, but Moore found his niche playing sports.

"It was more parks and streetball than anything else," he said. "We would travel from neighborhood to neighborhood and they would come to us. Football, basketball, baseball. It was like we had a league but the kids were running it."

He figured that basketball was his future because it was the game he loved the most. Moore was a legend at the the parks around Miami with nifty moves and cat-like quickness.

"But I stopped growing," he said.

Still, he was good enough to play both football and basketball at Miami Edison High and ran track as well.

He drew the attention of recruiters with his football talents, breaking decade-old rushing records when he rushed for 1,100 yards and 13 touchdowns.

"And unlike most of the areas of the state, we really prided ourselves in the Miami area on defense," he said. "So to do what I did, breaking the rushing record that had been there since the 1950s, that was quite an accomplishment."

Plenty of schools were interested in Moore during his senior year. Ohio State and Wisconsin were among them. Big 10 schools were turning to the state of Florida to improve their team speed and many of them thought Moore was exactly what they needed.

But there was one problem, a big problem.

"I screwed up my test scores," Moore said.

He was a non-qualifier which meant that going to any of the state powers or any Div. 1-A teams around the nation was not an option.

"That's why I spend so much time at schools today talking to kids about how important it is to understand what it means to be prepared for tests like the FCAT," Moore said. "It's not enough to do good work in the classroom. You have to be able to understand the tests and what they mean. It's work in the classroom, but it's also taking tests, and I try to get them to realize what they mean for their future."

Moore's football future in 1968 didn't look so good. At the last minute, he accepted a scholarship offer from Div. 1-AA Tennessee-Martin.

"I just wanted to continue to play football and go to school," he said. "And I wanted to get away from home."

Moore led the conference in rushing as a freshman and even played a game against Jacksonville State, which was coached by future Florida coach Charley Pell. But a semester away from home turned out not to be what he was looking for.

"It was the first year they had black athletes there, which was a little uncomfortable and I got a little homesick," he said. "My daughter had just been born back in Miami so I decided to come home and go to work. I had a daughter to support.

"But I didn't give up on football. The one thing I always felt was that I had been blessed with the skills to do something special. And that one year at Tennessee-Martin showed reinforced that I could play at that level."

To get back to football, Moore took a strange route—he started playing basketball again.

Moore drove a delivery truck by day and took classes at night for a semester. He enrolled at Miami Dade-South, a junior college in his hometown, to get his degree and play some hoops.

"The coach knew that I was trying to get back to football, to get to a major university, but that I would play basketball and try to help them win a state title," Moore said. "I set the record for assists because, even though I was a scorer in high school, I wasn't trying to get to a four-year institution in basketball. So I played point guard and made sure everyone else got the shots."

Bob McAlpine, the basketball coach at Dade-South, had played baseball with Florida coach Doug Dickey and let him know about Moore. But Big 10 schools were also hot on his trail once he received a degree from junior college.

Dickey convinced Moore to attend Florida.

"The worst-case scenario was that if it didn't work out in football I could play basketball," Moore said. "They only had one really good player—Tony Miller—at Florida so I knew I could play there. And really, I planned on playing basketball until things did work out in football.

"Wisconsin was on me big. They tried everything they could. They wanted to bring me and Rufus Ferguson together. He was from Dade County, too. But it was just too cold for me. Tennessee had been too cold, so I knew Wisconsin would be too cold."

Florida had also integrated its football program with pioneers like Willie Jackson Sr. and Leonard George.

"By the time I got there they had already gone through the growing pains," he said. "I went there really confident in my abilities. No matter who they had, I thought I could go in there and start. I had watched Miami practice and I knew I could play at that level."

At Florida, Moore was relegated to the scout team when two-a-days began. It didn't last long.

"They wanted me to give a picture for Fred Abbott and all of the guys on defense," Moore said. "They'd call a draw to the four-hole and I'd run up there, and there would be three linebackers waiting for me. So I'd cut it outside and run for a touchdown.

"I told Doug Knotts, who was the defensive coordinator, that the running backs in the game weren't going to just run it into the linebackers. So after I kept messing up their practice, they sent me to work with the offense."

Moore worked his way up to the second team where Lenny Lucas was the starting tailback. Florida opened the season with a game against Southern Methodist.

In the program for the game, No. 39 was listed as Nate Moore. He was an unknown to be sure.

But he hit the field for five plays, catching a touchdown pass in a 21-14 loss. The following week, Moore played a dozen plays in a 28-13 win over Mississippi State.

"Coach Dickey recognized my talent," he said. "He just told me to keep working and learn the offense."

Next up for the Gators was a trip to Tallahassee for a game against undefeated Florida State.

THE GAME OF MY LIFE
BY NAT MOORE

I've always felt that game against FSU was my signature game because it was an indication of my ability to make people miss. It kind of solidified people's recognition of my ability.

FSU was really good with Gary Huff and Barry Smith. They were 4-0 and had a bunch of seniors on their team. We weren't ranked and they were 13th in the country. But we went in there and kicked the living snot out of them, which is usually what we did against FSU.

Really, they were never in the game. Our offense could score at will.

It was so much fun to do that in Tallahassee where I still had so much family. They didn't recruit me either, and their coach, Larry Jones, said I couldn't play there. When people start to talk bad about you and they don't even know you, that stays with you. It made it that much more fun.

The leaders on that team—guys like David Poff and Fred Abbott and Ricky Browne—did a good job of getting everybody prepared mentally the day before the game, so we were prepared the next day.

I was even keeled before the game. I loved playing the game. You don't get paid in college so playing on Saturday, that's your payday. I didn't need any other motivation.

One of the highlight moments in Nat Moore's UF career came when he took a short pass and turned it into a 52-yard touchdown against Auburn. *University of Florida archives*

I was still the No. 2 running back. Lenny Lucas had been there and he had earned the right to be a starter. But it was still frustrating for me because every player wants to start. I had played a little more against Mississippi State. Coach Dickey was giving me more and more playing time, and that's all you can ask for is a chance to utilize your abilities. But the numbers I had been able to put up were limited.

Our defense kept getting turnovers and we kept scoring. In the first half, I had a 42-yard touchdown run where I made a couple of moves and went the distance. That was the thing—if you're not going to get a lot of carries you have to have one long run in the game to go over 100 yards. And it seemed like in almost every game I was able to break a long one. Even in the game before, I had a long kickoff return against Mississippi State but it was called back.

So I had that early touchdown, but that wasn't the one people talked about after the game. In the second half, we got down to about the 5-yard line, going in again against FSU. We ran a sweep to the right side. One thing about football is that you're not going to block everybody.

We did do a great job of blocking on the play, but there was one guy left unblocked. I was one-on-one with him in the hole. When you get into that position, you have to make the guy miss to make the play successful.

Usually on a play like that, the defender will try to force you inside because he has the sideline as a defender. But I made a sharp cut to the outside and he bit on it. I made a sharp cut inside, and he was reaching for air. He didn't touch me, and I went into the end zone untouched.

That play really solidified that if you get me one-on-one most of the time I'd win the battle. That came from all of those years playing sandlot football, making guys miss because there wasn't a lot of blocking. You develop certain skills from sandlot football.

I went over 100 yards in the game without a lot of carries because we just kept going down the field and getting turnovers. We won 42-13. Everything just kind of snowballed.

The game was validation for me in a lot of ways. It was special because I was from there and because of what their coach had said. I was kind of an unknown before the game, but after it was over, all of a sudden everyone knew who I was.

THE AFTERMATH

With Moore a bigger part of the offense, Florida went on to finish with a 5-5-1 record, beating Mississippi, Kentucky, Miami, and tying LSU. In that game, Moore made a 70-yard run to the 1-yard line, but Florida fumbled on the next play after Moore took a breather.

The 1973 season was supposed to be a big one for the Gators with Moore (who changed his number from 39 to 33), a Heisman trophy candidate. But first an ankle injury and then a knee injury robbed him of significant playing time.

"It was a tough year all the way around," he said.

The '73 team finished 7-5 with a Tangerine Bowl loss to Miami of Ohio despite 101 rushing yards from Moore on 16 carries.

The Miami Dolphins had seen enough of the slick running back to draft him in the third round as a wide receiver.

"Oakland and Dallas both wanted me as a running back," he said. "I was actually scared of receiver because it was something I had never played. But you have to take whatever opportunity presents itself."

Moore took the opportunity and ran with it, making the Pro Bowl in 1977. He retired after the 1986 season with 510 catches for 7,547 yards and 74 touchdowns.

His charitable works off the field also earned him the NFL Man of the Year Award in 1984 and the Byron White Humanitarian Award in '86.

Moore lives in Miami where he works for the Dolphins and is also the color analyst for Florida's television replays of all of its football games.

He also has established the Nat Moore Foundation which raises money for South Florida youth.

Chapter 24

BERNIE PARRISH

VANDERBILT AT FLORIDA
NOVEMBER 16, 1957
FLORIDA FIELD

PREGAME

In the 1950s, the best high school athletes were versatile to say the least. It's difficult to find one better than Bernie Parrish. In football, he was a two-way player at P.K. Yonge who once scored all of his team's 21 points in a big win over Williston. In basketball, he was the Most Valuable Player of the North-South All-Star game playing against a South team that included five starters who all went on to receive scholarships in college.

He was a star in track as well.

"They had outlawed the javelin for a while back then because someone got hurt and we instead had a football toss at the state meet," he said. "That was perfect for me. I threw it 60 yards and won easily."

And in baseball, Parrish once pitched back-to-back no-hitters.

"My high school coach Hank Bishop was the best coach I ever played for, and that includes Paul Brown and Blanton Collier," Parrish said. "He coached me in football, basketball, baseball, and track. Without him watching over me like a father while allowing me to play hurt and helping me to do my thing I would never have been successful in college or the NFL. Coach Hank allowed me to take over and dominate a game."

And he did in so many sports. Many people in Gainesville will tell you that despite all of the great athletes who have come out of the city— guys like Vernon Maxwell, Willie Jackson and Dale Van Sickel—Parrish may have been the best.

He believes it had to do with competition against Gainesville High.

"We were blessed in that way, the players at both schools, because any time we played in any sport we knew it was the best team we'd play against," he said. "I think it brought out the best in us."

When it came time to choose a college, Parrish assumed Florida would come calling. Instead, the football coach at the time—Bob Woodruff—called in four players from P.K. Yonge and told them they could walk-on at UF. One of them, fullback Tommy Bronson, went on to be an All-American at Tennessee.

"And beat the crap out of the Gators," Parrish said. "Woodruff told us we could live at home and they'd loan us some used books. Tom Nugent, the coach at Florida State, called Hank Bishop. He didn't have scholarships either, but he said that Dick Jones, one of the Florida assistants, said we didn't have the courage to play college football."

Parrish went to Florida despite the snub from Woodruff and the other coaches at Florida.

"I became a Gator despite the Gators," he said.

He was told that if he was good enough in baseball he could earn a scholarship in that sport.

"I was dumb enough to try to jam it down their throats," he said, "and take the scholarship out of their hides. I have no idea why he wouldn't give us a scholarship. There was no earthly reason."

Parrish thought about going to Stetson, even spending a couple of weeks on the campus in Deland, Florida.

"I looked at it but I didn't enroll in school," he said. "They offered me a scholarship. They told me I should come down there and be a big fish in a small pond. But I decided Florida was still the best place for me."

Parrish starred right away as a baseball player and earned that scholarship that put him on the football team the following fall. When he hit the field, he was handed jersey number 114.

Bernie Parrish enjoyed a career in the NFL and another in the field of building construction. *The Gainesville Sun*

"I won some coach fans like Coach John Ibner, Harvey Robinson, and John Mauer, who used to call a play in practice that called for me to lead block the defensive tackle," Parrish said. "Then they'd stand behind me and whisper to each other, 'Watch this. Watch this. Watch Parrish make that tackle spit blood.'

"Coach Hank Folberg would tell the defensive linemen to 'get after it or I'll run Parrish at you and we won't block you.'"

In 1956, Florida went 6-3-1 with Parrish playing right halfback and defensive back. The season was marred by a pair of losses to finish up. After a 28-0 win over Georgia that saw UF jump into the rankings at No. 13, the Gators lost 28-0 to Georgia Tech in Jacksonville and 20-7 to Miami.

"The only thing Woodruff said to me my first season was that my shoes were too big," he said.

The Gators were loaded for the 1957 season with players like Jim Rountree, Don Fleming, Jimmy Dunn, and Parrish, who had made all-conference that spring in baseball.

Florida opened the 1957 season with wins over Wake Forest and Kentucky. Those wins were followed by a crushing 29-20 loss to Missisippi State on homecoming.

Florida's win the following week over LSU put UF in the top 20, but a loss to Auburn a week later dropped the Gators out of the rankings. In Jacksonville, UF rolled over Georgia 22-0 and entered the Vanderbilt game with a 4-2 record.

Vandy was a strong team that was under consideration for the Gator Bowl when the Commodores came to Gainesville to face the unranked Gators.

THE GAME OF MY LIFE
BY BERNIE PARRISH

Vandy was on a roll. They had a really good team with Phil King and Tom Moore. They knew they had a shot at a bowl game and so did we. It was a big game, but every SEC game was a big game.

I played right halback and right cornerback. And I was a punter. Jimmy Dunn was a great coffin corner kicker but I would quick kick. That was our best play. I hit a couple over 80 yards, but in those days if you punted into the end zone they'd take 20 yards off your kick.

They were a really good passing team. Phil King was 6-foot-5, 230 pounds, and he was tough to handle. They liked to throw to him because he was taller than everybody else. And Tom Moore was a helluva runner.

Jim Rountree was a tremendous runner for us and usually I blocked for him. I resented that a bit because I knew what I could do when I got the ball. If I got it 10 times in a game that was a lot.

We didn't have a whole lot of strategy. Since I was at right halfback, I usually ran to the left.

They had a good team, but they didn't play very smart because they kept running around my end and I'd just stuff it. That was stupid.

It was a grind the whole game. I don't remember coming out because I punted and did some of the placekicking.

It was early in the second quarter and we were on their 45-yard line. The call came for me to carry the ball, and I had some room to the left after I took the pitch from Jimmy Dunn. I got near the sideline and thought I might have stepped out of bounds, but I kept running. I cut back when I got to the sidelines and had clear sailing. It was a 45-yard touchdown and we had the lead. I also kicked the extra point.

Later in the quarter, I had another touchdown run of 23 yards. I faked out Boyce Smith, left him grabbing at air. And again I kicked the extra point. That was just normal.

The second half was up to our defense. I had made a big tackle in the first half to stop a Vanderbilt drive deep in our territory. But we knew they were going to keep coming. They kept running it my way, and I kept making tackles.

But at the end of the game, we knew they were going to try to throw it to Phil King. Midway through the fourth quarter, I picked off one of Smith's passes on our 35 and ran it to their 45. But we couldn't get anything going on offense in the second half.

Late in the game, under three minutes, we were leading 14-7 and had to hold them. They were driving in our territory, trying to get the tie. They threw a pass into our end zone for Phil King and I knocked it down. All we had to do was run out the clock and I got 17 yards on one carry. They got the ball back with less than a minute to play and tried a deep pass, but Jimmy Dunn intercepted it and that was it.

Everybody was really happy. We couldn't go to a bowl game and that was kind of a wet blanket. But that was a nice win and knocked them out of bowl consideration.

For the game, I had 114 yards on 11 carries, played almost the whole game, and led the team in tackles.

I can't explain it exactly. There was a high school coach in Gainesville who said once that I had the ability to take over a game and run the other team off the field. That was just one of those games. It just happens. A few things have to go right for you to win a game like that.

The next week, I was honored to be named the national back of the week. There were some other great efforts and our whole team played terrific against Vanderbilt, but that was quite an honor. I still have the *Gainesville Sun* clippings from that game and the paper where I was named back of the week.

THE AFTERMATH

One would think that the national back of the week would be a focal point of the Gator attack the next game. Instead, Parrish carried the ball five times in a 0-0 tie with Georgia Tech.

"I was leading the team in yards per carry, averaging 6.5 yards every time I ran with the ball, and had just rushed for over 100 yards," he said. "And I got it five times in the next game. Wouldn't you think if you had a running back who just went over 100 yards you'd give him the ball 20 times? But I was right back to blocking for Rountree."

Florida was back in the rankings and finished the season with a 14-0 victory over Miami on the road to wrap up a 6-2-1 season. The Gators were on probation and couldn't go to a bowl game.

Parrish was featured in *Sports Illustrated* as a leading Heisman contender for the 1958 season. But he never got to that season. Instead, he opted to sign a pro baseball contract with the Cincinnati Reds.

"I had another year of football eligibility remaining, but they didn't want me," he said.

He played baseball for two years before going back to football with the Cleveland Browns. He flourished as a defensive back, being named defensive rookie of the year and helping his team win the 1964 World Championship.

In 94 NFL games, Parrish intercepted 29 passes and returned three of them for touchdowns. He played eight years in Cleveland and one with Houston of the American Football League.

In 1971, he wrote a controversial and much-praised book—*They Call It a Game*—which detailed the inner workings of pro football.

After retiring from football, Parrish went into the construction business building luxury hotels all over the United States.

Parrish retired from the construction business and moved back to Gainesville where he is an avid golfer. But he also continues to work against the system.

Parrish has organized a group of former NFL players who are working to improve NFL pensions.

Chapter 25

WAYNE PEACE

PREGAME

Although he has spent most of his life in Lakeland, Florida, Wayne Peace was born in Gainesville. His father, Lamar, was a fullback at Florida when Wayne was born. When he was four years old, the family moved to Lakeland where Peace immersed himself in sports.

"It was my life," he said. "I got sheer joy out of all of it. We were a working-class family so we didn't have any money. Sports was my leisure activity."

He spent so much time playing football, basketball, and baseball at a park in Lakeland that friends began referring to it as "the park that Peace built."

In that park was a basketball goal, and as a seventh-grader Peace decided he was going to dunk a basketball. For a year he tried every day, finally accomplishing the feat as an eighth-grader.

At Crystal Lake Junior High, Peace was a quarterback and linebacker and he took his skills to Lakeland High where he started at quarterback as a sophomore. That team was mostly sophomores and struggled to a 5-5 record. But by his senior year, the sophomores had grown together and the team reached the semifinals of the state championship where it lost to Pensacola Pine Forest.

By then, recruiters were interested in the muscular quarterback, but Lakeland coach Bill Castle didn't allow recruiting visits during football season. But it was difficult for Peace to make visits during basketball season because his hoops team was ranked No. 1 in the state.

"Bear Bryant visited from Alabama," he said. "He was after three quarterbacks—John Bond, Lance McIlhenny, and I was the third. But he also told me that if it didn't work out at quarterback, he thought I'd be a good linebacker."

That sentiment eliminated Alabama. Peace was interested in Florida, Florida State, and Tennessee. He visited Tennessee and fell in love with the scenery in the area.

"I loved it. We went to a basketball game and I loved when they played 'Rocky Top,'" he said. "The recruiter picked me up at the airport and I asked him what those white bugs were that kept hitting the windshield. He said they were snow flurries. So it was down to Florida and FSU."

Peace was very close to his family, and that was the deciding factor. Lakeland was a couple of hours from Gainesville, and it was another two hours to Tallahassee.

Still, he liked what FSU had to offer.

"My junior year, I was signed, sealed, and delivered to FSU," he said. "Florida's facilities were bad. But before my senior year, I went to Florida's summer football camp. I really liked Gainesville. And I just decided it would be a lot easier to get in the car and go home if I was in Gainesville. That really turned the tide."

Charley Pell had been on the job for one season at Florida, one dreadful 0-10-1 season, but was working the boosters to improve the facilities. Peace liked Pell, but also liked Bobby Bowden at Florida State.

"It would be easier for my family if I went to Florida," he said.

In the recruiting class of 1980, Florida signed four quarterbacks— Peace, Mark Massey, Roger Sibbald, and Dale Dorminey. A picture of the four with newly shaved heads appeared on the cover of *Bull Gator*, a Gainesville-based fan magazine.

But Florida had a sophomore quarterback named Bob Hewko and another in Larry Ochab who had been a part-time starter the previous year.

Wayne Peace completed 70 percent of his passes during his junior season at Florida. *University of Florida archives*

As a result, Peace found himself buried on the depth chart when he arrived at UF.

"I was way down," he said. "There was a lot of talk that since I was the biggest and strongest and the best athlete of the quarterbacks, I was going to linebacker.

"So I went in to Mike Shanahan's office one day. He was our offensive coordinator and a great coach. I told him that if that ever comes up, moving me to defense, I'm gone."

Florida kept Peace at quarterback, starting Hewko as the Gators began one of the biggest turnarounds in college football history. They hammered California in Tampa 41-13 to open the season, then blitzed Georgia Tech in Atlanta 45-12. After a 21-15 win over Mississippi State at home, the Gators found themselves ranked 19th in the country.

The Gators were back, and Pell was a hero. Hewko had taken Shanahan's vertical passing game and executed it with precision.

But on a sunny day in Gainesville, it all came crashing down.

The memories of 0-10-1 were fading as Florida got off to a 3-0 start with LSU coming to town. The Tigers were unranked, and Florida appeared headed to a special season.

But against LSU, Hewko suffered a season-ending knee injury. The Tigers had little trouble beating the Gators 24-7. Just like that, the magic had been sucked out of Gainesville.

When Hewko went down, Florida turned to Ochab, a plump quarterback with a strong arm. But he had little success against LSU. Late in the game, Peace came in for a few snaps.

"It was just my week," he said. "They had been rotating the four freshman quarterbacks with the varsity and it was my turn. So they just wanted to get me on the field. The game was pretty much over.

"I really was enjoying the whole college experience. Running out onto Florida Field was exhilarating. I threw a couple of passes, but the one thing I remember was a long pass I threw for Cris Collinsworth. It just barely missed. I remember thinking how cool that would have been to have hit a big play in front of all of those people."

The loss to LSU dampened the spirit of the Gator faithful who had been through a difficult '79 season but still kept packing in to Florida Field. To make matters worse, they'd have to wait two weeks for another game. Florida had an open week before a trip to Oxford.

The question on every mind in the Gator Nation was who would start at quarterback.

THE GAME OF MY LIFE
BY WAYNE PEACE

The coaches made the decision that it was going to be between Roger Sibbald and me as to who would start. I think they felt that they'd rather go with a young talented guy rather than go with Larry, who was a senior, who was not markedly better. They figured they might as well let one of the young guys play, let him develop.

Since we had that open week, they gave Roger and me equal snaps all week in practice. We were going to scrimmage on Saturday and they pretty much let it be known that whoever did better was going to start against Ole Miss.

I can't say I was better in the scrimmage. They were probably wondering what they were getting into. Neither one of us lit it up. But later in the week, they told me I was getting the starting nod.

We stayed in Sardi, Mississippi, the night before the game. Coach Shanahan made me get up in front of the offensive players and go over the Ole Miss defense. I had to know their heights and weights and tendencies. It was something he did throughout my career the night before a game. It was something he had done with Bob, too.

Coach Shanahan was such an amazing coach. As my kids play sports, I tell them anyone who could play under a coach like him would be fortunate. He was such a calming influence.

I was lucky that it was an early game because I was nervous. We had a 45-minute bus ride to Oxford, and when I get nervous, I get sleepy. I finished my breakfast and I remember Robin Fisher standing up and saying, "Even the food here is bad. Let's go kick butt and go home."

I got on the bus and fell right asleep. I remember Fisher waking me up when we got to the stadium. I'm sure everyone on the team was wondering what in the world was going on with this freshman.

Going out there for warm-ups was neat because here was a big SEC game and I was the starting quarterback. Their quarterback was John Fourcade, and I remembered watching him when I was in high school. I was watching him warm-up thinking how cool it is to be on the same field with John Fourcade.

We were going to water down the offense, run it a lot and not throw a lot of passes, let our defense try to win it. When you know you have a better team, it's best just to grind it out.

But I threw a touchdown pass early in the game. Unfortunately, I was scrambling on the play and I went over the line of scrimmage. So it was called back. My first touchdown pass and it was called back.

I ended up only throwing 10 passes in the game, completing four. Collinsworth caught two of them. He was a wonderful receiver. Our defense got three turnovers, and we moved the ball on the ground. I ran it some, too, got 39 yards and had a 14-yard run. James Jones and Doug Kellom ran really well. Doug was near 100 yards (93).

Brian Clark kicked a field goal and they matched it. But we kept controlling the ball and kicking field goals. Brian kicked five of them, two in the fourth quarter.

Something I remember about the game was a reverse we ran. I was bigger than their linebacker, Keith Fourcade, who was John's brother. I spun on the play and was supposed to block him. I took him out. They literally had to carry him off the field. The next day when we were watching film they played that over and over. That poor guy had to hear it from his teammates, how a quarterback took him out.

Because we ran it a lot, it was a very quick game. We just dominated. Brian's field goals were all we needed, and we won 15-3.

A couple of boosters had flown my parents to the game. I was excited to see them after it was over, just so happy to have been a part of it. Sports guys were my idols. When I was a kid in Lakeland and I watched games on TV, I always thought, "If I could just do that one day." When I went to a Gator game in the ninth grade, "If I could just run out on that field one day."

I remembered going to that game against Rice and Tony Kramer and Jimmy Dubose ran 80 yards on the first play. It's so vivid still I thought this is it. To now be a part of it was very exciting.

THE AFTERMATH

Florida went on to finish with an 8-4 record with Peace finishing the season at quarterback. Hewko returned for the following season and the two shared time the next two seasons as Hewko continued to have knee problems.

Peace had the job to himself in 1983 and had a wonderful season, but the Gators could not get past the same obstacle that haunted them in the 1960s and '70s—Georgia. Florida went 0-4 against the Bulldogs during Peace's four years, but had an overall record of 32-15-1 with bowl games in each of the four seasons.

In the spring of 1984, Peace signed to play with the Tampa Bay Bandits of the USFL. He was traded to Portland and remembers a conversation with Los Angeles Express quarterback Steve Young.

"He told me to get out of this league," Peace said. "And this was a guy being paid premium bucks."

Peace did leave the Portland team and took a shot at the NFL. But after training camps with Cleveland, Miami, and San Diego he decided he was finished with football.

"I've never been a guy who was defined by football," he said. "I was fed up with it. I went back to school to finish up and I was ready to get on with my life."

Peace returned to Lakeland and the local newspaper ran a story about him being retired from the game. The next day, three different companies called him to offer jobs.

He chose State Farm, which offered him his own agency. He opened the doors to Wayne Peace State Farm Insurance in February of 1987.

Peace still lives in Lakeland with his wife and four children. He recently marked his 20th year with State Farm.

"I always tell these young guys to use football to get what you want out of life," he said. "Don't let football use you up and throw you away."

Chapter 26

JOHN REAVES

PREGAME

John Reaves was typical for his time growing up in Tampa—an exceptional athlete who played everything. He starred in football, basketball, baseball, and track for Robinson High but it was football that drew the attention of the college recruiters. Reaves was named the outstanding player in the state in his senior year.

Tennessee, Georgia Tech, Florida State, UCLA, and Notre Dame all recruited Reaves, but there was little doubt in his mind where he was heading.

"I was a Gator fan growing up in Tampa," he said. "I'd read 'The Morning After' by Tom McEwen in the *Tampa Tribune* and it was always loaded with beautiful stories about the Gators. Florida State was always on the back page.

"I grew up a street over from (UF tailback) Larry Smith and there were some players from Robinson on the UF team. Don Brown was recruiting me, and I remember signing my letter at home. I still have it."

On the day he signed, Reaves had many visitors including McEwen, the longtime *Tribune* sports columnist, and Florida head coach Ray Graves.

"Rex Farrior Sr., who was a big booster, came over," Reaves said. "He drove up in this big Rolls Royce and asked me, 'Wanna take a ride, sonny?' Back then the boosters could recruit. You'd go to dinner all the time with boosters."

Reaves was a prototypical quarterback with size and a strong arm. Florida had produced a Heisman Trophy-winning quarterback in Steve Spurrier two years before Reaves' arrival in Gainesville.

But it wasn't like Graves had a wide-open passing attack.

"I can't think of any time when we went 3-wide," Reaves said. "It was always two wide receivers, tight end, fullback."

In those days, freshman were still four years away from being eligible to play college football, so Reaves settled into his role as the freshman team quarterback. There he developed a relationship with Carlos Alvarez, a wide receiver who was the son of Cuban immigrants.

The freshmen played four games against Auburn, Georgia, Florida State, and Miami, winning three and losing to Miami in Coral Gables 35-34. In scrimmages, the freshmen would go against the varsity team.

"There was one about two weeks after we started practice, a big scrimmage," he said. "We put 28 points up against the varsity. They were shocked. They couldn't cover Carlos."

That varsity team of 1968 was supposed to be one of the best in the country. It was proclaimed in the media as the long-awaited "Year of the Gator." But an injury to Smith and a seven-fumble performance by the Gators at North Carolina left Florida fans with another familiar slogan—Wait 'til next year.

In the 1969 spring game, the teams were divided up—young guys vs. the veterans. The young guys, led by Reaves, won 48-6.

After the spring game, Florida offensive coordinator Fred Pancoast walked up to Reaves and said, "You might want to stick around this summer. You might be the starting quarterback."

Florida had a returning starter in Jackie Eckdahl, a Gainesville boy whose father was a professor at the university. But the Florida coaches knew they had something special in their sophomore-to-be.

"I got a job that summer with the stadium crew," Reaves said. "We would sand off the numbers burned into the seats, then paint them over with slimmer stripes and burn in new numbers. They wanted to get more butts in the seats.

"That was a lot of sanding when it's that hot. I think we increased the capacity by three or four thousand. I remember the crew chief was this guy who every morning at 8 a.m. was ready to go. He smoked this pipe, barely lit, and when it would rain he just turned it over and kept working. We were getting $1.25 an hour, but we liked it."

Reaves did more than sand bleachers at Florida Field. He spent a lot of time watching film, most of it on Florida's 1969 season-opening opponent—Houston.

"The more you watched, the better you played," he said. "I've always been a big believer in that. After a while, I felt like I knew everything they were doing. They played a lot of man-to-man defense, their cornerbacks five or six yards off the receiver. If you play a team that doesn't throw, that's a good defense.

"And I hate to give the Seminoles credit for anything, but the tape of their game against Houston really helped because Florida State was the one team that threw the ball on them. I watched that tape a lot."

When practice began in the summer of '69, the offense had little trouble moving the ball against the Gator starting defenders. Two weeks before the game, Graves announced that Reaves would be the starter.

The final scrimmage came the Wednesday of the game. The starters beat the freshman and B-team players 93-0.

"That's when the coaches thought, 'We might have something here,'" Reaves said.

Houston was not the kind of first-game opponent a team with so much youth usually wants to play. With its veer offense and a star receiver in Elmo Wright, the Cougars had scored 100 points against Tulsa the previous year.

The Associated Press had Houston ranked seventh in the preseason. *Playboy* magazine was so enamored with the Cougars it picked them No. 1 in its preseason edition.

But the Florida players were confident because they knew they had a secret weapon. Actually, they had four. By the time the 1969 season was over, they would be dubbed the Super Sophs—Reaves, Alvarez, tailback Tommy Durrance, and fullback Mike Rich.

They felt they could score on anybody after dominating every scrimmage. Florida fans were a bit wary of a team that had let them down so many times before and was now starting a rookie quarterback.

The stadium was not quite full when the game started, but it looked like a million people were there to the wide-eyed sophomores.

"People said they sold tickets at halftime, but it looked packed from the start to me," Reaves said.

The night before the game, the team stayed at the Alachua Holiday Inn a few miles north of Gainesville. There, defensive coordinator Gene Ellenson gave one of his usually rousing speeches and explained how the defense was going to stop the veer by attacking the point where the quarterback has to make a decision.

The next morning after breakfast, Pancoast grabbed Reaves and Alvarez and told them to ride in with him.

"Well, what do you think?" Pancoast asked.

"I think we oughta throw the bomb on the first play," Reaves replied.

"Well, maybe not the first play but pretty early," Pancoast said.

The two kids could hardly wait.

THE GAME OF MY LIFE
BY JOHN REAVES

We won the toss and chose to receive. We wanted the ball. We started Jerry Vinesett at tailback and ran him twice for about three yards. That put the ball on the 26, right hash mark. And I made the call—79 streak.

I got to the line and looked up, and it was just what I expected. The cornerback was five yards off Carlos and the safety was covering the tight end. It just confirmed what I thought would happen.

I took my drop and when I hit my seventh step, I looked to where Carlos was supposed to be. He was five yards behind the guy. I just threw it down there like I had been doing for the last year and a half. Carlos caught it and nobody was going to catch him. It sounded like a bomb went off in that place.

It was surreal in there. You kind of looked around to take it all in, but we knew we had a lot of football left to play.

John Reaves threw 19 interceptions in 1969—nine against Auburn and 10 against everybody else. *University of Florida archives*

So they got the ball, and the first play they ran that veer, and just like Coach Ellenson said, we attacked that point where the quarterback would either pitch it or keep it. Jack Youngblood was a yard into their backfield and caused a fumble. So we were right back out there.

We had to settle for a field goal, and they didn't do anything and punted. We worked it back down the field and scored again and it was 17-0. It wasn't like we were surprised. We knew we could do that.

From there on, everything was working. We called a tight end around pass, and Guy McTheny threw a touchdown. And right before the half, Jimmy Barr picked one off and ran it back. It was 38-6 at the half. Houston, their players were faceless almost. We just kept doing all the things we had been doing in practice. We knew what they were going to do and they kept doing it. I think we had 500 yards of offense at the half.

Everybody was bouncing off the walls at halftime. The coaches were trying to calm us down, telling us we had another half. We knew that, and we couldn't wait to get back out there.

At one point, I was standing on the sideline with Coach Pancoast and he called the wheel route where the tailback goes to the flat and then turns up the field. He asked me who I wanted in there and I said, "Tommy Durrance." That was his first play of the game, and until the day of his death he always thanked me for that. Sure enough, it worked perfectly and he scored a touchdown.

When we came out for the second half, the whole student body was lined up, forming a tunnel for us to run through. Sometime in the third quarter, they pulled the starters when we were up 52-6. Elmo Wright scored a couple of late touchdowns to make the final 59-34.

Richard Kensler came up to me on the sideline and asked me if I knew I had thrown four touchdown passes. I didn't know. I was just playing.

THE AFTERMATH

Reaves remembers someone calling him after the game to tell him the *Prudential College Scoreboard Show* mistakenly had Houston winning the game. He knew better.

"It was a great and special feeling," he said. "I was lucky to be part of that. We had so many great players and what a tremendous coaching staff.

"It's funny because to this day people come up to me and tell me they were at that game."

Florida went on to win nine games for the first time in school history. A loss at Auburn—where Reaves threw a record nine interceptions—and a tie against Georgia in Jacksonville were the only blemishes on the record. The Gators capped the season by beating Tennessee in the Gator Bowl.

"I really believe that if we had known how good we really were we could have done even better," Reaves said. "We were ranked in the Bottom 20 before the season. Florida had always been beat down. We just didn't know how good we could be."

He also didn't know that a drastic change was in the works. Before the Gator Bowl game, word leaked that Graves was stepping into the athletic director's role full time and Tennessee coach Doug Dickey, a former UF quarterback, would be the next Gator coach.

The move caused dissension within the team, and Dickey's ball control style didn't fit Reaves' strengths. Florida went 7-4 and 4-7 in his final two years.

"He was stubborn," Reaves said. "We worked all the time on running plays. When we'd fall behind, we hadn't worked enough on passing the ball. Carlos was hurt, and we had a young line. I was running the veer. But I still treasure my time at Florida."

Reaves spent three years with Philadelphia before being traded to Cincinnati. He also spent time with Minnesota and Houston before going into the real estate business.

But a new league brought him back for more. The USFL's Tampa Bay Bandits, coached by Steve Spurrier, enjoyed success from 1983-85, with Reaves sharing the quarterback duties.

When the league folded, Reaves went back to real estate, but football called again. He served as quarterbacks coach for Spurrier at Florida for five years and also spent a year at South Carolina as an assistant coach before making real estate his permanent profession.

Chapter 27

LARRY SMITH

PREGAME

Larry Smith was born in Tampa and had what he called "a pretty typical" athletic career as a boy. Sandlot football, Little League baseball, a little basketball.

He was hardly the big tailback that would terrorize SEC teams for three seasons at Florida.

"I was kind of small to medium," he said. "I played all the sports, even a little basketball without much success."

Back then, there was no Tampa Bay Buccaneers, so the big thing every week in the fall was the Friday night high school football games. Smith loved going to the games and watching the bigger boys play the game he wanted to play.

"Friday night ball games were the biggest event in town," he said.

He attended Madison Junior High and played tailback. But it was between his ninth and 10th grade years that everything changed.

Seemingly overnight, Larry Smith grew up. He went from an unremarkable 5-foot-8 kid to a 6-1 strapping young man. The growth spurt couldn't have come at a better time, as he was getting ready to tackle high school football at Tampa Robinson, the team he had grown up watching on all of those Friday nights.

In his second game at Robinson, he found himself starting at tailback and he never left the line-up. After being a third-team tailback as a ninth-grader, he wasn't about to let the opportunity pass him by.

"Up until that point, I had all kinds of physical problems," he said. "I was always breaking my feet and hands. I had Osgood-Schlatter's disease which affects your bones. So I had a bunch of injuries, always beat up."

By the time he was a junior in high school, Robinson's football team was on the rise. The first-ever playoff game for the school was a state championship game against Coral Gables. Robinson lost on a last-second field goal.

By then, the recruiters had noticed the team's tailback and the letters came pouring in from SEC schools as well as Florida State, Miami, and Duke.

His senior year at Robinson saw the team fall back to a 5-5 record, but Smith was good enough to be named All-State and All-America. The recruiters kept coming to Tampa to see him play, and scholarship offers were not lacking.

"I was recruited pretty heavily," he said. "A lot of guys came to the house to see me. All of the coaches were great and all of the schools had a lot to offer."

But Florida had a strong pull. Smith's father had attended UF, and he had been going to games since he was a kid.

"There was a strong Gator following in Tampa," he said. "Everybody would go to the high school game on Friday night, the Gator game on Saturday afternoon, and come back and go to the Tampa University games Saturday night."

Filled with football, he still had a decision to make. Smith took recruiting visits to Duke, FSU, Auburn, Miami, and Florida. He was supposed to make a final trip to Vanderbilt, but he knew where he wanted to go.

"With my dad going to Florida and being a Gator fan all of my life, I was pretty partial to Florida," he said.

Ray Graves and his wife, Opal, also had made an impression on Smith, telling Smith's parents they would take care of their son in Gainesville.

So Florida it was, and his decision thrilled a lot of Gators in Tampa. They couldn't wait to see how their hometown boy performed on the big stage.

That would have to wait since freshmen were not eligible. Smith played in four freshman games, the team going 2-2.

"It didn't really mean anything," he said. "Going to Florida was pretty intimidating. It was my first time playing with a lot of guys older and bigger. It was, 'Go out and play there.'

"When I got there, they said we'd never practice with the varsity. And then they'd send you out there to get killed going against the varsity."

Smith moved into the starting tailback position as a sophomore on a team with high hopes. Spurrier was a senior starting quarterback and the team was loaded for a try at the school's first-ever SEC title.

Smith led the conference in rushing, but the Gators lost to Georgia to end any dreams of an SEC title.

"It was a good year, a fun year," he said. "It worked out well. It was a pretty good year for the University of Florida. I just wish we hadn't lost that game to Georgia and won the SEC."

Florida finished its season in the Orange Bowl against eight-ranked Georgia Tech. The underdog Gators pulled the upset thanks in no small part to Smith.

Backed up near the goal line and looking to get a few yards to punt the ball away, Spurrier handed the ball to Smith who found a gaping hole in the line. He cut to his right and sprinted 94 yards to turn a 6-0 deficit into a Gator lead.

On television, it appeared that Smith's pants were sliding down as he ran down the sideline for the score. Urban legend, he said.

"I had these plastic hip pads that were riding up on me," he said. "Everybody thought my pants were falling down. You can't run with your pants down.

"To be honest, that play was a bit of a fluke. They were in a goal-line defense and I popped through and there was nobody there. It was a thrill, though. We had a great time down there. The Orange Bowl people really treated us well."

In his junior year, Spurrier was gone along with several other key seniors. Florida went 6-4 with no bowl game, but Smith still had a productive year.

Larry Smith scored 27 touchdowns in his three years as Florida's primary tailback. *University of Florida archives*

"After Steve left," Smith said, "we had trouble finding our offensive identity."

The 1967 Gators did get revenge against Georgia—a 17-16 win—and were 6-2 after eight games, but lost to Florida State and Miami at the end of the season, scoring only 29 points in the two losses.

But in 1968, Florida was expected to be a force again. Ranked sixth in the preseason, it was supposed to be the Year of the Gator. Florida fans had heard that before, but this would be different.

It was. For four games.

Florida opened the season with four straight wins before the Year of the Gator came crashing down. In Chapel Hill, seven fumbles led to a 22-7 loss in the rain.

A tie against Vanderbilt and a loss to Auburn eliminated the Gators from the SEC race and knocked Florida out of the rankings. In Jacksonville in a downpour, Florida was humiliated 51-0 by Georgia.

The Gators edged Kentucky before facing Miami in the season finale in Gainesville. There would be no bowl game for the second straight year. This would be UF's bowl game.

THE GAME OF MY LIFE
BY LARRY SMITH

It was a frustrating year, a very disappointing year. The week before the first game I popped my hamstring and that bothered me the whole season. And then in the Vandy game I sprained my arch and that held me back. It was very painful.

It was just one of those years when I was never completely healthy.

But this was my last game playing for the University of Florida, and for all of us seniors there was a lot of emotion. Any time you're playing in your last game, it becomes very important to you.

I was still banged up, but I was going to play. This was my last college football game.

Miami had a very good football team. We knew it was going to be a tough game. And it was.

They had a tough defense. Ted Hendricks was playing for them and they had beaten us the last three years, including Steve's Heisman season.

Our offense didn't do a whole lot in the first half and they scored on a field goal in the first quarter and then a touchdown in the second quarter, so we were down 10-0 at the half. Our defense was hanging in there and we just needed to get something going offensively. Jack Youngblood was our kicker, and he had missed a long field goal.

I caught a few passes and ran the ball a lot, just kind of pushed the injuries aside. Tommy Christian had a couple of nice runs. We finally scored in the third quarter, Gary Walker from a yard out, to make it 10-7. And our defense gave us the ball back late in the game.

We drove it down there, got to the 6-yard line. It was an off-tackle play and they handed me the ball and I went off tackle, found a hole, and turned it outside. Just like in the Orange Bowl two years earlier, the blocking was great and I was fortunate to have the room to run.

I made it to the corner of the end zone for the touchdown. We ended up winning 14-10. It was a great feeling.

I didn't go back in the game when we got the ball again. I was resting (after 21 carries for 96 yards and three catches for 51 yards) and we were just sitting on the ball, running out the clock.

So that was my last carry at the University of Florida, a touchdown run to win the game. With the season we had, it was a nice way to finish my career. It was a great thrill to score the winning touchdown on my last carry ever at Florida.

The year had not gone too well, so it was nice to end it on a high note. Especially for all of the seniors.

THE AFTERMATH

His career at Florida over, Smith turned his attention to the NFL. He knew he would be a high draft pick and he was, taken in the first round by the Los Angeles Rams.

In his first season for the Rams and George Allen, Smith was the team's rookie of the year.

"The Rams didn't have too many rookies that season," Smith deadpanned.

But that team did start the season 11-0 with league MVP Roman Gabriel at quarterback. Despite losing the final three games, Los Angeles went to the playoffs.

For the next four years Smith continued to play for the Rams. But when Allen left for Washington, he traded for Smith.

Smith played only one season with the Redskins before hanging it up. The injury bug had followed him to pro football.

In his only season in Washington, Smith broke his hand, foot and leg.

"I was just getting too injured," he said. "It didn't make any sense to keep playing."

He finished his six-year NFL career with 2,057 rushing yards and 18 touchdowns rushing and receiving.

Rather than fight through more injuries, Smith decided to go to work. While in the NFL, he had earned a masters in business. He worked in Tampa in the banking industry and then spent two years working for the Tampa Sports Authority.

At the age of 30, Smith decided to take a new course of action. He went to Stetson law school and graduated with a law degree, then worked for a firm in Tampa for five years before moving to Hill, Ward, and Henderson in his hometown.

Smith has settled in Tampa and has been at Hill, Ward, and Henderson for 20 years as a real estate lawyer for the firm.

Chapter 28

STEVE SPURRIER

FLORIDA VS. AUBURN
OCTOBER 29, 1966
FLORIDA FIELD

PREGAME

It's a great trivia question that elicits more wrong answers than right ones—Where was Steve Spurrier born? It wasn't Johnson City, Tennessee, where he grew up, but in Miami Beach at St. Francis Hospital where his father Graham was a preacher. He was named Stephen in honor of the first Christian martyr and was the third child born to Graham and Marjorie, whose maiden name was Orr. Many years later, his closest friends would call him "Orr."

Two years later, the family would move to Tennessee, finally settling down in Johnson City when Spurrier was 12. By then, sports were a big part of his life as he started playing football in sixth grade and took ground balls from his father in the yard.

He was also an exceptional basketball player who scored 40 of his team's 44 points in a fifth grade game. It was as a child that Spurrier had the drive to win instilled in him by his father.

"He asked all of the kids how many of them thought the object of the game was not whether you win or lose but how you played it," Spurrier said. "When a bunch of them raised their hands, he said, 'Then why do you keep score?'"

215

That competitive fire fueled Spurrier in all of the sports he played. He had learned how to punt at the Kiwanis Park in Johnson City and was always playing pick-up games with older boys.

It wasn't until midway through his junior season at Science Hill High that Spurrier began to play quarterback. He had worked at his game, both as a quarterback and a kicker, using a plastic tee he received as a present to launch balls over a tree in the backyard.

Already, he was accomplished as a basketball and baseball player.

"I was better in those sports but I wasn't going to quit football," he said.

By the time he was a senior, he had grown and become more agile. The slow, awkward sophomore had become a polished senior quarterback, and the coach at Science Hill—Kermit Tipton—saw this and began to open up the offense.

He was also finding another sport that fed his competitiveness—golf. He'd sneak onto the Johnson City Country Club with a 3-iron and some old balls and work on his game.

Spurrier was an all-state football, basketball, and baseball player at Science Hill, pitching his team to two straight state titles. As a pitcher, he didn't lose a game for three years.

He was recruited by colleges to play all three. Fortunately for Florida, the word spread to Gainesville that Johnson City had an athlete that football coach Ray Graves needed to see.

Graves has told the story many times about his brother Edwin, who lived in Knoxville, telling him about the young phenom that Graves needed to be recruiting.

At the time, Graves had just completed his third season as the Florida coach. He was thinking about opening up his offense and needed a quarterback who could do more than run and hand the ball off.

"He came to Johnson City a couple of times," Spurrier said of Graves. "I had been to a few games at Tennessee, and everyone kind of assumed I'd go there. But they were still running the single wing, and I wanted to pitch it around, so that wasn't going to happen.

Steve Spurrier's love for calling his own plays led to his career first as an offensive coordinator and then as a head coach.
University of Florida archives

"I didn't visit Florida until after basketball season. It must have been April or late March. I wanted to see what it was like, and I thought I might play baseball, too. But I was going to major in football."

The weather in Gainesville couldn't have been better, even though Spurrier was fighting a cold on his visit. Graves used several carrots to try to lure Spurrier away from his home state. He told him he planned to start throwing the ball more. He took him to the golf course that the University Athletic Association had just purchased.

"One of the big things for me, and I used it in recruiting when I was the coach at Florida, is where do you want to live after you're through playing," Spurrier said. "All of these people were retiring to Florida and moving to Florida for a reason. The weather was great, the golf courses were great and they were going to run an offense that was suited to me."

Spurrier also liked Graves' honesty and the fact that he was also the son of a preacher.

In the end, Spurrier turned down Tennessee, Alabama, and Mississippi, along with others and decided to attend Florida, a decision that changed the football history of the school.

After playing on the freshman team in 1963, Spurrier was expected to battle Tommy Shannon for the starting job. When Shannon skipped spring practice to play baseball, it was Spurrier's show to run. Shannon was the starter for the opener, but Spurrier came in against Southern Methodist. The season had its ups and downs, including a botched field goal attempt against Alabama in a 17-14 loss when Spurrier misjudged the 7-yard line for the 2-yard line.

But the following year, Shannon was gone and the Gators belonged to Spurrier.

In 1965, he engineered a remarkable comeback against Florida State, hitting Charlie Casey for the game-winning score.

"They gave out the bids early back then for bowl games, and we already were going to the Sugar Bowl," he said. "We had a 16-3 lead on FSU, but they came back to take a 17-16 lead. We got it down to the 25. I saw one of their linemen jump early so I knew I had a free play. I rolled out and Don Knapp threw a great block for me so I was out there by myself. It was a free play so I waved Charlie down the field and took a shot."

Florida lost to Missouri 20-18 in the Sugar Bowl, but Spurrier was the game's Most Valuable Player, leading the Gators back from a 20-0 deficit. Florida's coaches went for two after each touchdown, leaving them on the short end of the score.

But it was Florida's first major bowl game and they had Spurrier coming back for his senior season. Great things were expected for the 1966 Gators.

Florida opened the '66 season with a surprisingly easy 43-7 win over Northwestern. On that day, Spurrier kicked a pair of field goals and threw three touchdown passes.

The Gators beat Mississippi State and Vanderbilt before pulling out a nail-biter against Florida State 22-19 in Tallahassee.

Unranked North Carolina State gave the Gators and Spurrier a scare in Raleigh. Spurrier drove Florida to the winning score, a 31-yard touchdown pass to Richard Trapp, to give Florida a 17-10 win.

UF then handled LSU in Baton Rouge 28-7 to run its record to 6-0. Next up was a critical game at home against Auburn.

THE GAME OF MY LIFE
BY STEVE SPURRIER

When people ask me about my favorite games as a player, two stand out. The first one was that 1965 game against Florida State, because we came from behind and won. The other is, of course, the game against Auburn, which a lot of people have said won the Heisman Trophy for me.

It was Homecoming and we were ranked seventh. They were having a so-so year, but it was a crazy game. We were going up and down the field on them and they had about 150 yards of offense. But they had some strange plays to stay in the game.

We scored first and they returned the kickoff 89 yards for a touchdown. And then they got the strangest touchdown of all. Back then, you couldn't pick up a fumble and run with it, but you could if it never touched the ground. Tommy Christian fumbled and the ball stayed on one of our linemen's backs. Gusty Yearout of Auburn grabbed it off the guy's back and started heading for our goal.

We were about to score and I was chasing Gusty Yearout down the field. I chased him for a while. I ran after him for about 50 yards and then Richard Trapp passed me, chasing after him. I said, "Go get him." But Gusty ran it 91 yards for a touchdown.

So even though we were dominating the total yards, they were leading at halftime. We were tied at the end of the third quarter and tied again late in the fourth quarter.

They couldn't stop us. Back then, you got to call your own plays, so I'd call it in the huddle and make it work.

They scored to make it 27-27, and we got the ball back with about four minutes to go. We moved it again, right down the field, and got to about their 20-yard line. But on second down, I was called for intentional grounding. Then it was third-and-30.

I hit Jack Coons on a little tight end delay down to their 23. That at least gave us a shot at a field goal to win it on fourth down.

We called time-out. I said to Coach Graves, "Let me kick it." It was out of range for our regular kicker Wayne "Shadetree" Barfield. I practiced a little during the week. People forget that I had made those two field goals against Northwestern in the opening game. I had missed one against N.C. State. So it wasn't like I had never tried a field goal.

I went over to the sidelines and put my square-toed shoe on. Some of the coaches were saying, "Let Barfield have a shot." But Coach Graves told me to go ahead.

It was 40 yards, which was just about my range. I hit it as good as I could. It came out straight and went right through to give us a 30-27 win.

A few years later, Forrest Blue was a teammate of mine with the San Francisco 49ers and he had been on that Auburn team. He told me, "We didn't know you were a kicker." If you watch the film of that kick, they didn't really rush hard because they were convinced we were going to fake it. But I had a feeling I could make it.

There were a bunch of sportswriters at the game and a lot of others found out what had happened. So that game probably did win the Heisman. It was a big win, but we still had a big game the next week against Georgia.

THE AFTERMATH

The big game against Georgia didn't go as well for Spurrier and the Gators. The Bulldogs won 27-10, harassing Spurrier throughout the game and returning an interception for a touchdown.

"*Sports Illustrated* came in that week and we had all this publicity," Spurrier said. "I had all of this publicity around me. We didn't know how to handle it.

"We forgot that we still had to beat Georgia."

Instead, Spurrier was denied the SEC title by the Bulldogs. It stayed with him as a coach and he made beating Georgia a high priority when he took over the Gators in 1990. In 12 games against the Bulldogs, Spurrier's teams were 11-1.

Florida finished its regular season in '66 with a loss to unranked Miami, but had secured a bid in the Orange Bowl against Georgia Tech. Florida won 27-12 against the eighth-ranked Yellow Jackets.

Spurrier then headed to the NFL, where he served mostly as John Brodie's back-up at San Francisco. He was the first quarterback of the Tampa Bay Bucs (they went 0-14) and his last stop was as a free agent in Miami. After he was cut there, Spurrier went into private business before resurfacing as a Florida assistant in 1978.

After giving the NFL a try with the Washington Redskins, Spurrier walked away from a big contract and took a year off. He wanted to get back into the college game and ended up at South Carolina, where his team has played in two bowl games and had two winning records.

He returned to Gainesville three times in 2006. Spurrier was honored with the 1996 national championship team and was put into the Ring of Honor along with three other players prior to the Alabama game. And he coached in The Swamp against Florida in a thrilling 17-16 victory for the Gators on their way to a national championship.

Chapter 29

COACH

STEVE
SPURRIER

FLORIDA VS. FLORIDA STATE
JANUARY 2, 1997
LOUISIANA SUPERDOME
NEW ORLEANS, LOUISIANA

PREGAME

Spurrier had made quite a name for himself as a player at Florida, engineering numerous late comebacks, guiding Florida to its first major bowl games and winning the Heisman Trophy. After a 10-year career in the NFL, he wasn't sure what he wanted to do.

He invested in an ill-fated athletic club, played a lot of golf, and wondered if there was a place for him in the game.

While attending a Florida game, the coaching bug bit Spurrier. Watching the Gators try to execute the passing game, he figured he knew enough about football to give it a shot.

Spurrier was hired by Doug Dickey in 1978 to be the Florida quarterback coach. One of the biggest things he did was move Cris Collinsworth from quarterback to wide receiver. But by '78, the Gator Nation had become sour on Dickey and he was fired.

New coach Charley Pell came in and immediately let go of Spurrier and offensive line coach Kim Helton. Spurrier still has the *Gainesville Sun* headline that reads, "Pell fires Spurrier, Helton."

Spurrier was hired at Duke to be the offensive coordinator where he worked magic with the Blue Devils' offense. That got the attention of

John Bassett, who was the owner of the Tampa Bay Bandits of the new United States Football League. He hired Spurrier to be his head coach, and Banditball became a big hit during its three-year run in Tampa.

When the league folded, Spurrier got the call from Duke again, this time to be the head coach. There, he pulled off the unthinkable, winning an ACC championship. He let it be known from the first play as Duke's coach that things were about to be different when he called a double-reverse pass.

During the 1980s, Florida kept bouncing in and out of a state of turmoil. An NCAA investigation forced Pell out as the head coach and put Florida on probation. Galen Hall seemed to right the ship, but eventually the sanctions leveled by the NCAA took their toll on Hall's teams. Even the arrival of Emmitt Smith couldn't make UF a contender in the SEC.

In the middle of the 1989 season, an investigation into the basketball program spilled over into football. Two small infractions were uncovered and that was the school's excuse to dump Hall and start looking for a new coach. Gary Darnell, the defensive coordinator, handled the team for the last seven games of a 7-5 season.

Spurrier met with UF officials, but did not want to take the job until both Duke and Florida had completed their seasons. Nor did he want to lie to the media about it.

"I told them that when our seasons are over, if you still want me to be the coach at the University of Florida, I'd like to take that job," he said.

Both Florida and Duke finished up with bowl losses while the speculation was running wild. On New Year's Eve, 1989, Spurrier was officially introduced as Florida's new coach.

His first order of business was to rip off the artificial turf on Florida Field. His second was to let it be known that there would no longer be any excuses for Florida not being as good as anyone else.

Then, he set about the task of making believers of the Gator Nation. It didn't take long.

In the first game against Oklahoma State in 1990, Florida came out throwing the ball all over the place. Spurrier's teams would shatter almost every Florida passing and receiving record, but most importantly the Gators shed their image as underachievers and instead would move into the elite of college football.

The only team to ever go 12-0 in the regular season ended with a whimper. In 1995, the Gators beat all comers until the Fiesta Bowl when they were thrashed by Nebraska 62-24.

Steve Spurrier's 122 wins at Florida averaged out to 10 wins per season.
The Gainesville Sun

So heading into the 1996 season, there was reason for optimism hedged with a little bit of concern.

The Gators started with a pair of easy victories, then went to Tennessee and scored the first 35 points of the game before winning by six. Over the next five games, Florida put on one of the most amazing displays in college football history.

The Gators beat Kentucky, Arkansas, LSU, Auburn, and Georgia by a combined score of 261-37. It was at Arkansas when Spurrier was heckled by a fan who accused him of running up the score.

"We like it when y'all say that," Spurrier said, flashing a No. 1 from his right hand.

The Gators had been No. 1 since the win over the Vols and appeared headed for the national title. A close call against Vanderbilt, when Danny Wuerffel had to pick up a fourth-and-1 late in the game to secure the victory, set the Gators up for the showdown in Tallahassee between No. 1 Florida and No. 2 FSU.

The Seminole defense was all over Wuerffel, and FSU pulled out a 24-21 victory. Reidel Anthony caught a late touchdown pass for UF that Spurrier would later say might have been an important factor in getting Florida to the national title game.

But the Gators were licking their wounds after the loss to FSU.

"We didn't even practice Monday," Spurrier said. "We watched the tape, and I told the players to go home, quit crying and bitching about the loss, and let's go win an SEC championship. That's what really matters."

But it was Spurrier who was complaining. He brought several media members to his office to view tape of all of the late hits Wuerffel had suffered. He went public with his anger and FSU coaches responded that they hit "until the echo of the whistle."

Still, Florida had an important game to play. In an offensive showdown, the Gators prevailed 45-30. Earlier in the day, Texas had stunned Nebraska, meaning Florida would get another shot at FSU if they could win the SEC. Once they did, the rematch was set for the second time in three years in New Orleans. This time, a lot more was at stake.

THE GAME OF MY LIFE
BY COACH STEVE SPURRIER

We lost a lot of seniors from that 1995 team, so it was a different team in 1996. Chris Doering, Jason Odom, Reggie Green, Mark Campbell, Ben Hanks. They were all leaders and really good players.

It's funny because Brian Schottenheimer actually threw the first touchdown pass of that season against Southwestern Louisiana. I was mad at the offense so I put the second team in but left Ike Hilliard in the game. Schottie threw him a little hitch and he broke some tackles and scored.

The next week was the week I kept Danny away from the media. He hadn't played well and I just wanted him to think about what he had to do. He kind of looked at me funny like he always did and then went out and was 16-of-17 against Georgia Southern.

We got it going after that Tennessee game. They had some chances to come back on us but we held them off and then we kind of took off.

But after we lost to FSU, I thought we were finished as far as the national championship went. A lot of things had to happen and they all did, including us beating Alabama.

At the Sugar Bowl, we decided to take the team out of town to Gonzalez the night before the game, just to get away from everything, which we started doing after that. We were all together and Arizona State was playing Ohio State, and if Ohio State won, we would be playing FSU for the national championship.

So I told the team to go watch the end of the game and then we'd meet back for dinner. Of course, Ohio State won late, and you could hear this big loud cheering throughout the hotel.

We met and I told the guys, "For some reason, God has put the game in our hands." Four games had to go our way, and they all did.

At the end of the meeting, we had everybody line up and shake hands and promise to play their hardest. That's all we wanted was everybody playing hard.

We had a different game plan only in that we went to the shotgun. We knew what they were going to do, blitz us just like they did in Tallahassee. But the shotgun let you get the ball off. They kept blitzing and we kept getting it off. I think after that game (FSU defensive coordinator) Mickey Andrews quit blitzing so much.

It's pretty easy to move the ball when you know what the other team is going to do on defense.

I don't think the things I said about them hitting Danny late really had much influence on the game. It was sad the way those SEC refs called the game in Tallahassee. I just felt like a coach has to stand up for his players when they are wrongly treated. They got a couple of personal fouls in this game, but really it was two things—the shotgun and the fact that our two tackles were healthy. Zach Piller and Mo Collins couldn't play the first time we played them, so we had Cooper Carlisle, a sophomore, trying to block Boulware and those guys.

As usual, we had a whole bunch of plays. Danny audibled a bunch in. To me, the play of the game was when we were up 24-20. We were at their 1-yard line and ran off tackle and we let a guy through who got Terry Jackson. And then we had a delay penalty. So it was third-and-8, Danny threw to Ike and the middle linebacker should have knocked it down. Danny got hit right after he let it go because our right guard whiffed. And Ike caught it and the defensive back could have tackled him, but he hit him high and Ike scored. Big, big score right there. Danny said he wasn't sure after he threw it if the linebacker was going to pick it off, and I told him I saw the same thing because I watch the secondary.

Danny ran one in. Then Terry made that long run. The funny thing is we scored on the same play the next year against FSU with Fred Taylor. That touchdown by Terry made it hard for them to come back. And we only threw once in the fourth quarter.

The best team doesn't always win the national championship, but I think we were the best. If you had an eight-team playoff, I think we would have won it.

THE AFTERMATH

Most of the players and coaches partied through the night before showing up for a press conference the next morning where Florida was presented with the appropriate trophies. Spurrier wanted to make sure the votes were all in, as if the 52-20 win wasn't convincing.

"People ask me why we didn't win any more national championships," he said. "We just didn't have the same kind of leadership. And we didn't have Danny Wuerffel anymore."

After two seasons with the NFL Washington Redskins, Spurrier decided he'd had enough of the pro league and took a season off, playing golf, spending time at the beach, and watching his son Scotty play. He shocked Florida fans by taking the job at South Carolina, where he already has proven to be a thorn in the Gators' side.

"I'm still a Gator," he said. "I just work for another school."

Chapter 30

DANNY WUERFFEL

FLORIDA VS. FLORIDA STATE
JANUARY 2, 1997
SUPERDOME
NEW ORLEANS, LOUISIANA

PREGAME

Growing up, Danny Wuerffel was always on the go because his father was in the Air Force. Every three years the family would be uprooted and moved to another part of the country.

"I think it helped me in some ways," he said. "And as an athlete it was always easy for me to make friends."

Just before his freshman year of high school, there were two options for the Wuerffel family—Japan or Fort Walton Beach, Florida. Who knows how the future of Florida football might have been changed if it had been Japan. But it was Fort Walton Beach, a football-crazy town.

Wuerffel had played quarterback in seventh and eighth grades in Colorado and stepped right into the slot in Fort Walton.

"I was actually a better basketball player," he said. "It was certainly different in Florida. We had a jamboree and I had never played a night game before, especially in front of that many people in the stands and cheerleaders and hearing my name announced.

"I went into the game and totally forgot the play the coach had called. I started calling plays from my team back in Colorado."

229

Wuerffel recovered to be a back-up quarterback as a sophomore who also kicked and punted. When Jimmy Ray Stephens arrived from Williston High to be the head coach, the two clicked. Wuerffel became the starter and led Fort Walton Beach to the state title as a senior.

He had grown up a Florida State fan and those closest to him thought he might end up as a Seminole rather than a Seminole-tormentor.

"It came down to Florida, Florida State and Alabama," Wuerffel said. "I visited all three. From a quarterback perspective, it really came down to Florida and FSU. There were two things that made me decide on Florida.

"One, Coach (Steve) Spurrier had so much success; and, two, if I weren't playing football there was no question I'd have gone to Florida. It's funny because my sister was at FSU and I actually went to more of their games when I was in high school. I was naturally and emotionally tied to Florida State. But I wanted to think this through. I leaned on my mind."

After a redshirt season, Wuerffel burst onto the scene in his second college game, throwing a strike to Chris Doering for the game-winning touchdown at Kentucky.

The following week against Tennessee, Wuerffel was brilliant in a 41-34 win. He started the next four games as well, but in Jacksonville against Georgia struggled with a wet ball. A flustered Spurrier put Dean back in and he pulled out the win. Dean would start the rest of the season, winning the SEC title and the Sugar Bowl.

Dean was again handed the ropes to start the 1994 season, and Florida was ranked No. 1 in the preseason polls. After scoring 70 points in the first two games and putting a 31-0 whipping on Tennessee at Neyland Stadium, the ranking looked justified.

But before a home game against Auburn, Spurrier told Dean that he wouldn't hesitate to pull his quarterback if he struggled in the big game. His confidence shaken, Dean did exactly that. Wuerffel came into the game and started the remainder of his career.

As a junior, Wuerffel had an incredible group of receivers—Ike Hilliard, Reidel Anthony, Chris Doering, and Jacquez Green—and the Gators were almost unstoppable. Wuerffel threw 35 touchdown passes, and Florida rolled through the regular season unbeaten. The Gators played a rare game in Athens, Georgia, against the Bulldogs while the stadium in Jacksonville was being renovated and became the first opposing team to score 50 points there. They scored 48 points in a row against Tennessee, put 49 on Auburn and scored 63 on a cold, windy night in Columbia, South Carolina.

When the Gators beat FSU for the first time in five games and handled Arkansas 34-3 in the SEC Championship Game, they were off to their first ever national title game. But in the Fiesta Bowl, Nebraska showed why it may have been the best team in college football history by dismantling the unbeaten Gators 62-24. The Cornhuskers blitzed Wuerffel all night, and the beating he took got Steve Spurrier to start rethinking the possibilities of putting his quarterback in the shotgun.

When the 1996 season began, Florida certainly had the talent to get back to the title game, but the schedule included games at Tennessee and at FSU. Florida scored 35 points in the first 20 minutes in Knoxville and held on, then blitzed through its conference schedule with Wuerffel at the controls.

The stretch against LSU, Auburn, and Georgia was particularly impressive when UF outscored those three teams 154-30.

With a berth in Atlanta secured again, the top-ranked Gators headed to Tallahassee for an enormous game against No. 2 FSU. It was a physical, emotional game with the Seminoles prevailing 24-21 on a field filled with sand and potholes. But the controversy wasn't about the sorry state of the field as much as it was about Wuerffel.

A few days after the game, Spurrier was livid about the number of late hits Wuerffel took against FSU. Little did he know that a rematch was just around the corner.

"Nobody was really thinking about that," Wuerffel said. "The overall mood was that we had made another great run and that loss had ruined it. There was a lot of frustration among the players and the coaches. It was a real test for the leadership and our senior leaders really got the team on track for the SEC Championship."

Florida won that game in a shoot-out over Alabama 45-30 as Wuerffel threw six touchdown passes. Earlier in that day, Texas had stunned Nebraska meaning the Gators would get another shot at Florida State in the Sugar Bowl. When that game ended earlier in the afternoon, the players exploded in their hotel rooms. They wanted another shot at the Seminoles, this time on a neutral field.

And when they beat Alabama, the bowl game had a chance to mean a little more.

As the week of the Sugar Bowl rolled on, Spurrier never backed off his criticism of Florida State's style of hitting quarterbacks. FSU coach Bobby Bowden countered by saying his players hit "until the echo of the whistle." One of the great rivalries of college football had been racheted up even higher by all the rhetoric.

It would get even more intense.

The night before the Sugar Bowl, Arizona State lost to Ohio State. The Sun Devils went into the game unbeaten, and the loss meant Florida and FSU would be playing for it all. Gator fans celebrated on Bourbon St.

But they still had to find a way to beat the 'Noles.

THE GAME OF MY LIFE
BY DANNY WUERFFEL

I tried not to personalize myself with the whole situation about the late hits. Coach Spurrier wasn't trying to blow it out of proportion. He just believed what he saw. My dad told me after the first Florida State game that he had counted the number of times I was knocked down and it was 32 times. It felt like it.

But it was different going to the Superdome rather than going to a place where they had a huge home-field advantage. We had been to New Orleans before, in 1993 and '94, so it was a place we were familiar with.

Plus, we had been to the national championship game the year before and got caught up in the hype so we knew how to avoid it the next year.

So we felt pretty comfortable with the situation. We knew the stadium, we knew it wasn't going to be a hostile crowd, and we knew how to handle all of the stuff leading up to the game.

The night before we played in the Sugar Bowl, we went to Gonzalez, Louisiana, just to get away from everything and take a real business-like approach to the game. We knew what we had to do and we also knew we

The Gainesville Sun **selected Danny Wuerffel's 114 touchdown passes as the No. 2 record all-time at UF.** *The Gainesville Sun*

had a new plan that included putting the shotgun in to give me more time to get rid of the ball.

Everyone knows what happened the night before with Ohio State winning. We knew what it meant. There were a lot of guys yelling and screaming but we also knew none of it mattered if we didn't take care of our business. So after we met with Coach Spurrier, it went back to being very serious.

The thing I remember about that game was the play Ike Hilliard made. I threw the ball to a spot and got hit just after I let it go so I didn't realize what had happened until I looked at it on the big screen. He timed up the catch so he could grab it and then just slam on the brakes. Both guys went flying by him and he ran it in. It was a phenomenal play by Ike.

There was another big play to Ike where I had no time to get rid of the ball down by the goal line. I threw it, got hit, and started to get up pretty quick because I knew I was going to be chasing down the linebacker. I was afraid he was going to intercept it. I was hoping the ball would sneak in there to Ike and fortunately it did. I'm not sure how. The linebacker was in the passing lane and the cornerback was hanging all over Ike.

We kept it going on offense. The shotgun was working, and our defense was playing an excellent game. Late in the third quarter, all of the receivers went to the left and I was looking that way when I realized it was wide open to the right. So I just took off for the corner of the end zone. I was lumbering as fast as I could. I always had dreams of diving into the end zone just inside the cone. I wasn't the most athletic guy in the world, but it happened right there.

That was about the time we started feeling pretty good about things. And then Terry Jackson broke that run in the fourth quarter and that pretty much sealed the deal. It was an amazing night.

It was kind of bittersweet for me because here we had done the thing we had set out do, won the national championship and there were so many media members I couldn't find any of my teammates to celebrate with. I remember running all over the place trying to find my teammates and I was being chased by the media.

That night was pretty exciting, but we also knew it was the last time we'd all be playing together. What a way to go out. It wasn't just that we won it, it was the way it happened. Losing to FSU and then getting another chance.

THE AFTERMATH

The following morning it became official when the polls came out that Florida had won its first national football title. The players, many of whom had stayed up all night, showed up for a press conference at the New Orleans Hyatt.

A week later, the team was honored with an amazing celebration at Florida Field, where 70,000 fans showed up.

Wuerffel went on to be a fourth-round draft pick, ironically enough by New Orleans. He played six seasons in the NFL passing for 2,123 yards in 25 games but never enjoyed the success he did in college.

After retiring from football in 2003, Wuerffel continued his work with the Desire Street Ministries in one of the roughest neighborhoods in New Orleans. Hurricane Katrina forced the Wuerffels out of the city in 2005, but Danny set up shop in Destin, located the families and children he had been working with and is moving his school to Baton Rouge.

"As great as that game was and that season was," he said, "Three out of every four people who come up to me talk about how thankful they are for what I'm doing now."

Chapter 31

JACK YOUNGBLOOD

**FLORIDA VS. GEORGIA
NOVEMBER 7, 1970
GATOR BOWL
JACKSONVILLE, FLORIDA**

PREGAME

Jack Youngblood's family was living in Fernandina Beach, where his grandfather was the sheriff of Nassau County for 20 years, when it was time for him to come into the world. He was born in Jacksonville and lived in Fernandina Beach for the first four years of his life.

The family moved to Orlando where his father went to work with one of Youngblood's uncles in the funeral business. When he was eight, Youngblood and his family moved to Monticello in Jefferson County, 25 miles from Tallahassee.

Already, he was like most kids that age, playing sports year-round.

"It's what all the boys did," he said. "We were all war babies and we'd play home-run derby in the summers, touch football in the falls, and basketball in between. There was no Pop Warner in Jefferson County. You just got together and played. We even played dodge ball, trying to kill each other.

"There were just natural activities we got into. And everybody in a small community just gravitated together."

Youngblood was good at football, but really excelled in baseball.

"I could hit the curve ball," he said. "Played first base. I enjoyed that."

It wasn't until the sixth grade that he started playing organized sports, making the junior varsity team and playing anywhere he was asked to play. But playing sports had turned out to be a painful proposition for Youngblood.

He was growing faster than his body could handle. His tibia and femur bones in both legs were advancing rapidly and the rest of his leg couldn't keep up with them. As a result, he developed a problem in his joint line and calcium knots formed in each leg.

"It was the most painful thing," he said. "You couldn't even wear jeans it hurt so much. A doctor told me, 'You don't need to be playing with those things.' He wouldn't let me finish the season (in sixth grade).

"I just wanted to get through it, keep going until I got to the next stage in my growth pattern. And it did get better. But it was pretty tender. I remember getting hit in my right knee and, oh, it felt like I was shot. But I never thought about quitting. I just wanted to get through the thing. I think that's when I first discovered I had a little determination."

Sitting out games as a sixth-grader was frustrating for Youngblood. At 5-foot-10, he looked like exactly what his team needed and heard it from teammates. By the time he entered high school, the pain had vanished and his body had grown into itself.

He was still scrawny, but wiry. He joked that he had to run around in the shower to get wet, but by his sophomore year he was becoming a force on defense at middle linebacker.

Offense was another story. With only 20 players on the team at Jefferson County High, everybody had to go both ways. As a senior, Youngblood and his teammates were greeted by new coach Brett Hall.

"We had been together, all of us kids, for four years," Youngblood said. "We had a pretty good little team. But Coach Hall brought the cohesiveness we all needed.

"I was playing center and middle linebacker. The first game of the year, the other team had this little nose tackle. I was playing center and I was chasing him around the whole game. I don't think I've caught him

Jack Youngblood is the only player to be in the NFL Hall of Fame and the Florida Ring of Honor. *University of Florida archives*

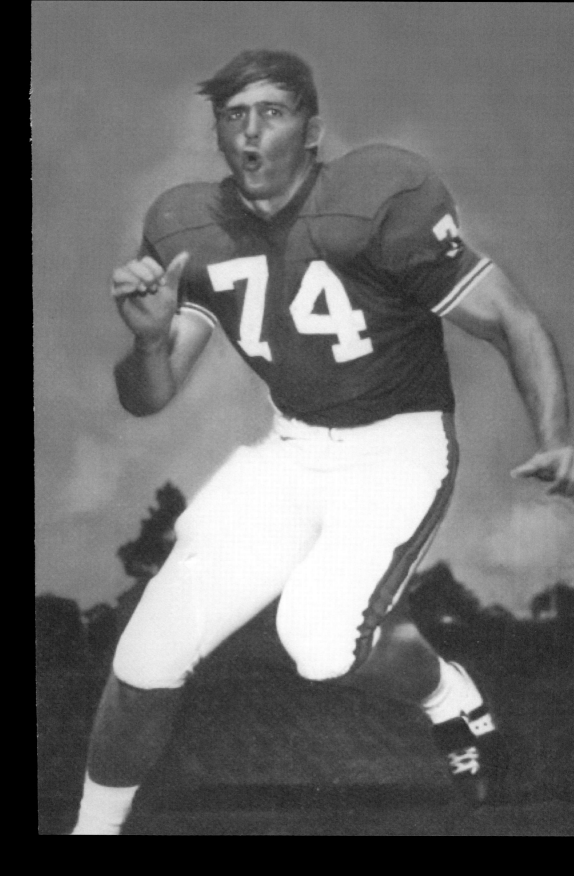

yet. He was all over the field. But he wasn't making any tackles because I kept yanking him down his jersey. I think I had five holding calls in the first half. Coach Hall sat me down. I haven't played another offensive down since.

"At first, my feelings were hurt. But then I realized it was a real opportunity. I was the only player who got to play on one side of the ball."

Jefferson County won the state title in Class B that year and the offers began pouring in for Youngblood. Well, not really.

There were none. Nobody was recruiting Youngblood during his senior season. This was long before the Internet and the recruiting fever, and in Monticello it wasn't difficult to be unnoticed.

One coach did notice. After the state championship game against Avon Park, a meaty hand grabbed Youngblood by the arm.

"We were hooting and hollering and jumping all over the place," Youngblood said. "This guy grabs me. It was Dave Fuller, who was the baseball coach at Florida and helped with football recruiting. I had no idea who he was. He asked me, 'How would you like to play for the University of Florida?' I said, 'Yessir.' That wasn't a hard question to answer.

"I had planned on going to North Florida Junior College. Florida was my one and only offer."

Although he lived 25 miles from the Florida State campus, the Seminoles were not interested. They sent assistant Bill Parcells, whose evaluation of talent would improve later in life, to Monticello. He told FSU coach Bill Peterson that Youngblood would never play college football.

"When we get together at an outing," Youngblood said, "Parcells holds court with that story."

At 6-foot-4, 200 pounds, Youngblood was tall for a middle linebacker and light for a defensive lineman. Florida coaches tried him on the offensive line. He wanted to play middle linebacker. Eventually, defensive end became his position.

He played on the freshman team in 1967.

"If we lost to FSU, we had to cut our hair," he said. "So we definitely didn't lose to FSU. I really wanted to play middle linebacker. They had Mike Kelley there, but I didn't care. I never shied away from competition.

"They moved me to the line and I walked around pouting for a week. I was so disappointed. Middle linebacker is the quarterback of the defense. They kept moving me around. They finally figured I couldn't play strongside end at all. My style was too high. But I did have a quick step off the ball."

Youngblood was up with the varsity in 1968 and was even the kickoff man for the Gators. His first kickoff in the season opener was returned for a touchdown by Air Force.

"I was thinking, 'This isn't a great start for my college career,'" Youngblood said.

It got better.

Although the 1968 season was a disappointing one for the Gators, Youngblood was starting to fill out and was getting comfortable in his position as a weakside end. He was one of the main players on a defense that was overshadowed on Florida's 9-1-1 team of 1969.

But before his senior season, Florida made a coaching change. Ray Graves was out and Doug Dickey was in.

It would make for an interesting senior year.

Dickey's Florida career did not exactly start off with a bang. After a narrow win over Duke in Jacksonville and a rout of Mississippi State at home, 13th-ranked Florida was thrashed by Alabama in Gainesville 46-15.

Youngblood had suffered a knee injury in the Duke game and had missed the next two games. He returned to help the Gators beat North Carolina State, Florida State, and Richmond, but a loss to Tennessee was followed by the ultimate in humiliation.

On Homecoming, Florida lost to Auburn 63-14.

"It was a miserable day," Youngblood said. "And it meant we weren't going to a bowl."

There was only one thing that could salvage Dickey's first season—a win over Georgia.

THE GAME OF MY LIFE
BY JACK YOUNGBLOOD

The season was a difficult one for everybody because we were going through this transition to a new coach and we all loved Coach Graves.

There were definitely some disgruntled players on the team going all the way back to the preseason.

I think the thing that had bothered everyone the most was that we hadn't been included in the decision-making. We had such a good season in 1969 and felt like we had a big stake in the 1970 season, especially seniors like me.

Coach Graves had been like a grandfather or a father to us. He could be hollering at you and the next he has his arm around your neck, all within three minutes. Coach Dickey was very business-like in his approach to things.

So even though there were high expectations and we were ranked to start the season, there was a whole bad tone at the start of things.

Then came Auburn.

That was just terrible. We couldn't do anything to stop Pat Sullivan.

So there weren't a lot of people giving us much of a chance the next week against Georgia. But Georgia is different. It's a tradition that is passed on to every team, every year. It's an honor to play in a game like that.

So all week, it was like, "Forget everything that is happened. Forget the Auburn game. Let's go perform. We're not going to a bowl game. Let's go get our own reward."

That was our way of overcoming all of the adversity we had been through. Go beat Georgia.

And you have to remember, not only had they tied our great team from the year before, but when I was a sophomore they beat the doggie doo out of us. That (51-0) was the worst loss of my entire career. And it stayed with me.

So now it's my senior year, things aren't going well, we're 5-3 and not going to a bowl game and it's Georgia. With all of the turmoil, we all had to dig down deep.

And we knew it was going to be a knockdown, drag-out slugfest. We were going to have to force some turnovers because our offense was struggling getting used to the new style Coach Dickey had brought in. But he had kept the 4-3 defense that Coach Graves ran, which was good for me. Coach Graves had gone up to Atlanta with his assistants and they had schooled for three or four days with the Falcons one off-season.

They had two really good running backs and they kept trying to pound the ball down the field. Ricky Lake went for over 100 yards against us in that game and Robert Honeycutt had 99. They didn't throw much, but in that game we only threw once in the first half.

Their quarterback, Paul Gilbert, ran for one touchdown and Lake got another one so we were down 17-10 and they were driving to put the game away. We had to come up with a goal-line stand, and in the end that's what won it for us.

Lake was a tall kid, kind of an upright stance, stood up in the hole. He came into the hole and I saw I had a chance to get the ball away from him.

I just snatched the ball out. He didn't fumble it, I ripped it away from him. If I wanted to, I could claim to have been the instigator of that kind of play. They all do it now. Nobody tackles anymore. It's all slapping and grabbing.

So I ripped it out and the ball was just there on the ground. I jumped on it. Our defensive left side had done the job. You know you've done good when you look down and your butt's in the end zone, they're about to go in and you get the ball.

We went right down the field in two plays and scored. John Reaves hit Carlos Alvarez with a long pass to tie it. I was just hoping they'd keep the ball longer than three plays. I was trying to catch my breath.

And then we got the ball back and scored again to win it.

It was a great victory for us to have been so close to being down two touchdowns and then coming back to win it. That's the game I'll always remember because it was Georgia and after what they had done to us my first two years, it was special to beat them as a senior.

THE AFTERMATH

Florida finished the season with a 7-4 record after a win over Kentucky and a one-point loss to Miami. Youngblood was the 20th pick of the first round and went to play for the Los Angeles Rams.

He made such an impression the Rams traded Deacon Jones away and Youngblood was a starter by his third season. He played 14 years with the Rams and was best known for playing in the Super Bowl with a broken leg.

"There was some pain, but I wasn't going to miss that game," he said.

Sacks weren't an official statistic until 1982, so the record books show Youngblood with only 24 of them. But an unofficial count using game films puts that number at 151.5 sacks for his career.

Youngblood remained in California and had one of the first syndicated radio shows in the nation at a station in Sacramento. He worked with the World League franchise in that city in 1991 before moving to Orlando as one of the owners of the Arena League team there.

He sold his share of that team in 2000 and settled in Orlando.

Youngblood has settled in Orlando where he owns a company involved in software as well as an ethanol company.

"You can say I'm an entrepreneur," he said, "but I'll have to get the spell check to make sure it's spelled right."

Chapter 32

AHMAD BLACK

**AHMAD BLACK
FLORIDA VS. PENN STATE
JANUARY 1, 2011
OUTBACK BOWL
TAMPA, FLORIDA**

PREGAME

Ahmad Black was born in Orlando, Florida, and lived there until halfway through his kindergarten year. His father, Bruce, moved the family back to Lakeland where Bruce had grown up to be closer to ailing family members.

Bruce was a fireman who worked 24 hours on and then had 48 hours off. He made the commute when he was on and also was in the Army Reserve on weekends.

Black took a liking to sports right away.

"It was tough a little bit when we moved to Lakeland because I was a kid in a new school and it was a little bit different," he said. "I started playing sports in the playgrounds on Orlando where all the kids were bigger than me. Mom didn't want me to play but Dad made her let me. I came home crying a few times."

He was like a lot of kids playing multiple sports—football, basketball, soccer, baseball. When he turned six he began playing city league football. By the time he was ready for high school, Black had turned into an athletic but undersized football player.

He played at Lakeland Kathleen his first two years of high school despite pressure from Lakeland High to attend that school. His father had gone to Kathleen, so Kathleen it was.

After his sophomore year his coach, Richard Tate, left for a school in Haines City so Black transferred to Lakeland High.

"Kathleen was more of a basketball school that just happened to have good football players," Black said. "Lakeland High was a whole different animal. That was the first school I had been to that had boosters. They had their own football facility. There were a lot more people at the games."

Through it all, Black stayed grounded because of his parents.

"They were always telling me to stay in school," he said. "I lived in a rough neighborhood and it would have been easy to get persuaded to go the wrong way. They just kept me with a level head and kept me off the streets."

This transition was also easy because so many of the players at Lakeland High were guys he has played with in Little League—Mike and Maurkice Pouncey, and Chris Rainey. The Pounceys, both eventually first-round NFL draft picks, were identical twins who were tough to tell apart.

"I used to see what color shirts they were wearing and remember them that way," Black said. "Now I can tell them over the phone."

Lakeland High went unbeaten in each of the two seasons Black played there. He also played basketball.

"I didn't want to play but the coach was like, 'What size shoes do you wear?' They kind of persuaded me to play. Lakeland wasn't that good in basketball. We kind of turned it around, me and a couple of other guys."

Black didn't play basketball his senior year because he enrolled early at Florida. That was not where he expected to go during the recruiting process because Florida was not recruiting him.

On a team that didn't lose a game for two seasons, there were plenty of prospects.

"It was amazing because at any given practice we had 15 scouts watching," Black said. "It was crazy. Every morning at first period we'd go to the locker room and there would be letters stacked two or three feet tall. We'd sit in our locker and hand them out. Then, I'd get home and there would be more mail. I opened a lot of them but only to see if they were offering."

Florida wasn't one of them. Ohio State and LSU were both recruiting Black heavily and he was ready to commit to LSU because a teammate – Jordy Hammond – had committed to the Tigers.

"They were hounding and hounding me," Black said. "But when I called to commit, they said they'd have to pull a couple of scholarships and they'd get back to me. Maybe they didn't think I'd commit. Maybe they were hounding me to get someone else."

The next day, a contingent from Lakeland went to Florida's summer camp. Black had to be persuaded to go. He performed well and UF coach Urban Meyer offered him on the spot. Take it or leave it.

"Rainey was in my ear to take it," he said. "So I took it."

The next day, the Pounceys committed. In all, seven players from the Lakeland Dreadnaughts ended up as Gators that year. Some called them the Lakeland 7. Others referred to them as the Gatornaughts.

But things did not go well for one of the Lakeland 7 when he went through his first spring practice.

"It was terrible," Black said. "I came in thinking it was like high school. It wasn't. I'm covering Bubba Caldwell, Percy Harvin, Louis Murphy."

On Black's first day of school, Florida had won the national championship. Now, Florida would try to repeat. Despite Tim Tebow winning the Heisman that year, Florida struggled defensively and lost four games. Black played mostly on special teams.

But by 2008, Black was a big part of the team. And he made one of the biggest plays of a championship season.

In the national title game in Miami against Oklahoma, Black stole a deep pass from Sooner receiver Juaquin Iglesias in the fourth quarter that stopped a Sooner drive and started the game-clinching drive for the Gators in their 24-14 win.

"I don't think I could do that if I tried again," Black said. "Urban almost choked me when I came to the sideline. He wanted to make sure I caught it because they were reviewing it. 'Are you sure?'

"He was in the slot and I had one-on-one coverage with no safety help. I was tired because they ran that hurry-up offense. You could hear their coaches yelling, 'We got 'em. They're tired' That was the fastest offense I ever played against.

"The gameplan was that if they checked out of something we'd change our defense, too. But it was rough. Carlos Dunlap, when they'd get ready to hike it would hit the ball so they'd have to reset it so we could rest."

With Tebow back, Florida was ready to try to repeat the following year and went undefeated going into the SEC Championship Game against

Alabama. The Tide had been practicing for Florida all season and ruined the Gators' dream of playing in the Rose Bowl.

"Guys on team were making plans for California," Black said. "Alabama should have lost three games that year. They had a great gameplan for us. They wouldn't rush up the field so Tebow couldn't run. And we lost Carlos (to a DUI) the week of the game and I think that cost us the game."

Before Florida was to play in the Sugar Bowl, Meyer resigned as coach. A day later, he changed his mind. Florida steamrolled Cincinnati in the Sugar Bowl.

In 2010, Tebow was gone along with eight other players drafted into the NFL. It showed. The Gators lost at home to LSU and Mississippi State, then suffered an embarrassing loss at home to South Carolina with a return trip to Atlanta on the line. To finish up the regular season, they saw their six-game winning streak against rival Florida State snapped.

The offense without Tebow was anemic as Florida tried to play three different quarterbacks.

"I played hard every time I took the field," Black said. "A couple of guys played hard but not everybody."

They would play in the Outback Bowl in Tampa's Raymond James Stadium but before that could happen, Meyer resigned again. The Outback Bowl would be his last game.

THE GAME OF MY LIFE
BY AHMAD BLACK

I really wanted to win the game for Coach Meyer. But I wanted to win it for us seniors, too. That's what I was thinking about going into the week of the bowl game.

It had been a tough season. We lost at home to Mississippi State 10-7. How do we lose a game at home giving up only 10 points? I don't want to blame just the offense, though. It was just a tough year.

It was my last game at Florida and I was going to make it count. All week in practice, the coaches were giving me a hard time. Coach Meyer would walk by me and say, "Too small." We'd just laugh about it. Coach [Chuck] Heater, my secondary coach, would walk by and say, "Too small and too slow."

I thought a lot that week about the fact that I had come a long way. I was told I would never play at Florida. I was told I was a package deal to get some of the other Lakeland players. At the end of the day, I was one of the best ones.

We had some guys on the team, I wasn't sure how hard they were going to play. They were the ones who came in to the program in 2008 and had played in a national title game as freshmen and then the Sugar Bowl as sophomores. And now they were in the Outback Bowl? We had to be sure everyone was ready.

If it's a game I'm ready to play. I'm ready to play if it's Charleston Southern.

We watched Penn State on film and we knew they were going to come right at us. They didn't do anything fancy. Kind of reminded me of Alabama. If we couldn't stop that, I don't know what to tell you. We base our program on toughness and this was going to be a game of toughness.

We were pounding in full pads every day. We never did that during a game week. It was a Wednesday and the offense decided they weren't getting off the bus to practice if we were going to be in full pads again.

They were texting us and calling us and saying they were not getting off the bus until we're just in helmets and shorts.

So now, everybody on the defense is looking at me. I sat down and started chilling. We couldn't practice if the offense wasn't out there.

Maybe 30 minutes went by and the bus driver was ready to take them back to the hotel. The coaches came over to the defense and said, "Let's go." And we said, 'Naw, man, we're just chillin.'"

We were worn out. We couldn't take another day of full pads. Finally, Coach Mickey Marotti comes over and blows his whistle and says, "You've got five minutes to get out there with helmets on. So the offense got off the bus and we took off our pads and had practice in helmets only.

We were just having some fun. We have some characters on our team.

I made the first tackle of the game on the kickoff and we got a three-and-out. And then John Brantley throws an interception on the first series for the offense. The next few plays we had some mental breakdowns. I had one, too. I missed my guy.

We were already down one cornerback in Janoris Jenkins [with a shoulder injury] and then [cornerback] Jeremy Brown gets hurt. So it's going to be a tough day.

I grabbed my first interception of the game on a tipped ball and ran it back 49 yards to set us up for what should have been an easy score. But Trey Burton fumbled down on the goal line. I should have scored on the return.

My whole goal when I get an interception is to return it all the way. People think I'm kidding around but I hate to be tackled. I like tackling but I hate to be tackled.

We would have been in control of the game but there were two plays where we caused a fumble and they didn't give it to us. Didn't even review the call. On one, I stripped the guy. Urban was screaming at them to review it. There was a kickoff where they fumbled and they didn't give it to us, too.

It was a tough game. On one pass, I hit the receiver so hard I made him drop it, but I broke my helmet. The chin strap snapped in half. I was bleeding after that hit but I went back in the game.

The game went back and forth but we finally took the lead late at 30-24. They got a good kickoff return from their up back and I was thinking this is like the national championship game all over again. It's up to the defense to win the game.

I was trying to get guys fired up in the huddle. We had to stop them and get this one for Coach Meyer and the seniors.

Joe Paterno knew we were expecting them to throw it and they were running draw plays. They were moving it right down the field.

And then the play happened. I was lined up in the middle of the field and their tight end went in motion. Usually, we would have sent Josh Evans with him but we did something different and I stayed with him.

They crossed a receiver with the tight end and I baited the quarterback. I trailed the tight end until the quarterback threw it and then I cut in front of him.

I couldn't believe he threw it. It was a good break on the ball and I grabbed it and took off.

Now everybody says I'm not fast but I'm fourth all-time at Florida in interception return yardage. And I never got caught from behind. Never.

But I didn't think I'd score on this one. I thought they had the angles on me. But Jaye Howard blew up one of their linemen and the quarterback wasn't going to get me so it was wide open.

I looked behind me and there was nobody. And 80 yards later, I had a touchdown. There were 55 seconds left in the game. My last game and I clinched it with an interception return with less than a minute to play. That's a nice way to finish it up.

The great thing is I was running into the end zone where all of my famiy was sitting. I had 25 tickets to that game. I mean, it's 30 minutes from my house to the stadium.

When I looked at the replay, I saw the ref running behind me making sure I didn't celebrate.

I didn't want a dogpile because I would have died. I wouldn't let my teammates tackle me. The worst dogpile I ever saw was Will Hill against Georgia. His helmet was turned sideways and he couldn't breathe. I didn't want that happening.

Their quarterback threw five interceptions in the game and I could have had two more. I dropped one and was off balance on another I could have had.

Coach Marotti gave me a big hug and told me it couldn't have happened to anybody better. That felt good. Coach Meyer have me a big hug. And then he tried to get me to go out there for kickoff. That wasn't happening.

Someone told me they gave the MVP to someone else. I was thinking, OK, I had two interceptions and returned one for the clinching touchdowns and led the team in tackles and someone else is MVP?

But then they gave it to me, it's at my mom's house. She says it's her trophy. She won't let me touch it.

THE AFTERMATH

Black finished his Florida career with 13 interceptions which is the fourth most in school history. At 5-foot-10 and 184 pounds, he was hardly prototypical of an NFL strong safety, but he was selected in the fifth round of the 2011 NFL Draft by the Tampa Bay Buccaneers, whose home stadium is where Black played his final game as a college football player.